Horse Tales
for the
Soul

Compiled by: **Bonnie Marlewski-Probert**
Written by: **Horse lovers from around the world**
Edited by: **Susan Stafford**
Cover by: **Kristen Spinning, Kromatiks**

3onnie's other books and videos are available at finer bookstores and
;hops around the world, or by calling 800-700-5096. You can also order t
/ia the web at http://TheCompletePet.com

'Debugging Your Horse,"
.SBN# 0-9646181-1-7 $23.95
'A Parent's Guide to Buying that First Horse,"
.SBN #0-9646181-0-9 $16.95
'Debugging Your Horse," (video)
.SBN# 0-9646181-3-3 $32.95
'Trail Riding, Rules of the Road," (video)
[SBN# 0-96461814-1 $29.95
"Horse Tales for the Soul, Volume One"
[SBN# 0-9646181-5-X $19.95
"Horse Tales for the Soul, Volume Two"
[SBN# 0-9646181-6-8 $19.95
"Horse Tales for the Soul, Volume Three"
[SBN# 0-9646181-8-4 $19.95
"Horse Tales for the Soul, Volume Four"
ISBN# 0-9740841-0-7 $19.95
"Horse Tales for the Soul, Volume Five"
ISBN# 0-9740841-1-5 $19.95

The cover was designed by Kristen Spinning of Kromatiks in Tucson Ariz
Photographs were supplied by the authors and by Kromatiks.

Dedication

Horse Tales for the Soul, Volume One

I would like to dedicate this book to my loving husband Keith, and to the very brave authors within who openly shared some of the most cherished stories in their lives with me and in turn, with you. Keith is the most supportive husband in the world!

The idea for this book came from a letter that I received from Melonie Brewer. I had written a column about one of my school horses and in response to that story, Melonie wrote to me about a special horse in her life. It was a wonderful story. Later that week, I received another letter from a reader who sent me his story and in his personal note he added, "I knew you would understand." Both stories touched me so deeply that I wondered, how many other people are out there who have similarly uplifting, heart warming, wonderful stories and have just never shared them with someone else?

When I decided to actually put this book together, I wrote a letter to Melonie Brewer to let her know how important her letter had been and the results of that letter. A few months later, I was in Kentucky speaking at Equitana USA and after one of my talks a very beautiful woman approached me with her husband...it was Melonie Brewer. It is rare in life that you get to meet the people who have touched your life profoundly and even rarer indeed that you get to tell them. That was a very special day for me and even though Melonie couldn't have known how important her letter was, she would know after the book was finished as will you when you read the stories in this book.

We learn from every good and from every bad experience we go through. *Horse Tales for the Soul, Volume One* is intended to help you learn to laugh more often, be more sympathetic to those around you and to recognize that you are never the only person going through anything. There is always someone else who understands exactly what you are going through, you just haven't met them yet. You will meet many of those people between the covers of this book. I hope you will come to cherish each of them as much as I do.

Bonnie Marlewski-Probert, 2001.

Table of Contents

I ♡ horses

Horse Tales for the Soul, Volume One

Dedication 3
Introduction 7

Horse Tails   Pat Lynch 8

Chapter One, The Miracle Of The Horse

A Gift Of Love   *Sandra L. Costa* 10
The Great Spirit Horse   *Sandy Hart* 13
Cowgirl Dreams Do Come True   *Krystal Mincey* 16
4th Of July Surprise   *Meredith Hodges* 19

The Great Christmas Tree Fiasco   Susan Stafford 22

Chapter Two, The Intelligence Of The Horse

For Every Backyard Horse   *Elizabeth C. Gathright* 25
Tough Guy   *Laine Raia* 27
Andalusian Mare   *Susan Grindell* 29
Suffering For Our Mistakes   *Pamela Michella* 31
Clifford Goes To Camp   *Nancy J. Bailey* 34

Stinky   Mona L. Malone 37

Chapter Three, Overcoming Adversity

Lucky Icicle Blue   *Julie Anne Hurd* 41
Letting Go Of A Dream   *Melissa Merkle* 45
Beauty   *Michele Smith* 47
The New Horse   *Kathleen Monan Castro* 50
A Dream Comin' True   *MaryAnn Schafer* 54
Springtime Is My Favorite Time   *Emily Lineberger Bridges* 58

Mescalero   Cherry Hill 65

Chapter Four, A Love So Strong

I Was There For The Seasons Of Life   *Maia Bottemiller* 70
Memoirs Of A Perfect Partnership   *Lara Schwartz* 74

Blackie *Peggy A. Gwin* 77
Diablo, My Best Friend *April Douglas* 81
Elizabeth And Ginger *Bonnie Marlewski-Probert* 83
Itsy Bitsy *Megan K. Gravett* 88

Brumby Barbara J. Linsley 90

Chapter Five, Gratitude

Amigo Mio *Lynne Swank-Wilder* 95
Learning From Horses *Ron Meredith* 99
A Person Who Influenced Me *Jonalee Kagels* 102
They Earned A Good Retirement *Roxene Ballard* 104
A Modern Day Roundup *Joan McCallister* 107
The Perfect Pony *Staci Layne Wilson* 110

A Trainer in Training Bonnie Marlewski-Probert 116

Chapter Six, Saying Good-bye

Partners, A Horseman's Prayer *Ted W. Land* 119
The Horse Of My Dreams *Su Davidson* 122
Forever, Little Bit *Sandi Every* 125
Saying Good-bye *Sherri L. Pasquale* 127
Raindrop Will *Kris Robison* 132

The Door Annie Cuthbert 137

Chapter Seven, New Beginnings

J.J. *Alissa Ricci* 139
Rusty Was My First Horse *Dale J. Fraza* 142
Misti *Mandy Soter* 146
April's Easter Dawn *Melinda Strimback-Pepper* 149
One Or The Other *Mona L. Malone* 152
Dreams Can Come True *Cecily Bradley* 155

Introduction

Horse Tales for the Soul, Volume One

What lives between the covers of this book is the love, affection, good humor and trust that all horse lovers share with their four-legged friends. The authors you are about to meet have been gracious enough to share their personal stories with the rest of us.

For those of you who have been fortunate enough to have a special relationship with a horse, pony or other equine in your lifetime, you will see your own life in the stories that follow. After you read this book, you will be a part of the lives of every author. You will have shared in a moment in their life that has changed them forever and I trust it will change you as well.

When I decided to compile *Horse Tales for the Soul*, I could not have imagined what was to follow. As any responsible writer will do, I came up with an idea, faithfully acted upon it, moved forward, and waited to see how it developed. On rare occasions in a writer's lifetime a project seems to take on a life of its own and *Horse Tales for the Soul* has done just that.

Whether the story came from a nine-year-old or a prominent attorney what I noticed was that their lives may appear on the surface to be as different as night and day, but the reality is that they are more alike than they are different.

It has been an honor and a privilege to be entrusted with the fortunate task of sharing these stories with you. I hope you will enjoy them as much as I have and I recommend you invest in a large box of tissue before you begin!

Horse Tails

Horses have been a big part of my life and I showed them for a number of years. Back in those Good Old Days, horse showing (for me) meant entering as many classes as possible, with the hopes of making enough prize money to cover the expenses.

I had been trying for several years to come across a good buggy horse, as there was some fair money up for grabs in those classes. I bought an old Hackney mare at Brandon Spring horse sale this particular year. Not having anything better, I decided I would show her in some driving classes.

There was only one problem. Lady's tail was docked - cropped off short - and the classes in which I wanted to show her required a full tail.

Well, most of the farm folks are ingenious and "where there's a will, there's a way." I figured I could make a false tail for her and be able to show her in those classes where all the prize money was. Right?!

We had a lot of horses at the time, so I robbed some long hair from a few tails and made Lady a false tail. My mother thought I was crazy, and so did everyone else, but Lady was starting to look pretty good and show season was starting.

The first class Lady and I entered was a lady's driving class. I tied on Lady's tail and donned a long skirt (in one of my rare attempts to look like a lady). I asked my sister Inez and my friend Geraldine to stand outside the ring and if anything happened they were supposed to come to my assistance.

I must mention that Lady was probably 20-some-years-old and her tail had been docked since she was a baby. Now, what do horses use their tails for? Among other things, swatting flies. Well, this was one thing I didn't think about, but Lady did!

We got through the driving part just fine, but had to stand in a lineup before the judges gave out the placings. It was about 85 degrees Fahrenheit and there were quite a few flies around. Just about that time, Lady found out she had a fly swatter on her back end and, not having been able to get those pests for 20 years, she really was enthusiastic about it. To my horror, she swished her tail right off.

Here I am, trying to look dignified in a Lady's driving class and not wanting to draw a whole bunch of attention to my dilemma. I started frantically waving to my sister and my friend and pointing to the tail on the ground. Well, this was just too much for both of them and they stood there laughing their heads off. In fact, they were both laughing too hard to come and retrieve Lady's tail for me. I finally gave up on their help, hoisted up my floor-length skirt so that I could get out of the buggy, and retrieved Lady's fly swatter myself.

My brother says I won that class; I think I got third place, but it was the last time that Lady ever lost her tail. (P.S. This is not a false tale.)

Pat Lynch

Biography - Pat Lynch. "I have been involved with horses most of my life. I started riding to school when I was five-years-old and graduated from that to showing, racing and raising registered Quarter Horses. Most of my involvement with horses, at this point in my life, is through my art. I enjoy doing animal portraits and action scenes involving horses. I feel very fortunate to have had the opportunity to share many rewarding times with the horses that have influenced my life, and I am pleased to be able to share some of these with others." You can reach Pat at 204-752-2071, or at Box 164, Dundee Str., Alexander, MB, Canada, R0K 0A0.

The Miracle of the Horse
Chapter One

A Gift Of Love

Twenty years ago, I was approached at a show by a young couple who had a paralyzed 12-year-old daughter that loved horses. They wanted to pet one of my ponies, but they were afraid she would get hurt.

I had a beautiful three-year-old Shetland Pinto pony mare named Patience that I was showing. She was so gentle and sweet, and very, very smart. This little girl would beg her parents to pet or ride the pony every time she saw one. I asked her if she had ever ridden a pony. She said no, but she always wanted to. I asked her father if she could sit on Patience. That little girl's eyes lit up and she begged her Dad to let her. Patience laid her head in this child's lap and let her pet her ears, face and eyes. Everywhere the child touched the pony, she never moved.

Finally, her father lifted the little girl up on Patience's back. It was an instant connection. The little girl was petting Patience and the mare would put her head back and smell the girl's legs and just stand quietly. The little girl begged her parents to have a pony, but they didn't think the child could take care of one and they were also concerned for her safety while spending time around such an animal.

I took the parents aside and talked to them about training this pony to lay down and let the girl get on her. Can you imagine the look I got from them? They said if I could do that then we might have a deal, but the pony had to be safe.

The first part I had seen done on a TV show and thought "how hard could it be to teach a horse to lay down on cue?" The second requirement concerning safety was no problem, as this mare was bomb-proof! But boy, was it a challenge to teach this mare to bow! I worked faithfully for five months to help this little girl realize her dream. She never suspected what plans we had for her and Patience.

On Christmas morning, I pulled up in the trailer, took Patience out and stood by her beside the trailer. The parents wheeled the little girl out to the truck and showed her the Christmas gift. Patience bowed gracefully, went down on both knees, then down on her side. The little girl got herself out of her wheelchair, dragged herself over to Patience and hugged her, tears running down her face. The mare had been trained by voice command and with a little hand whip, which made it easy for the child to learn to cue her.

As the parents stood there watching, I cued Patience as to what to do and the child did all the work herself to get on. Patience then rolled onto her side, the girl threw her leg over the saddle and hung on. Patience very carefully got up on both knees, then one at a time, lifted that child until she was standing. With words of encouragement, and tears streaming down all our faces, she made it! You should have seen that little girls' eyes light up when she realized what she had done. She realized that she had legs again and could walk.

I had designed a special strap that hooked onto the saddle and buckled around the horn so there was no way she could fall off. The saddle didn't need stirrups, so we took them off. Later, they put them back on and used rubber bands to keep her feet in the saddle so that she could show the mare. Yes, she even showed Patience in riding classes and won a blue ribbon in Western Pleasure. Nobody knew she was paralyzed once she was on that pony. She rode like a champion - and that is what she was. She rode that pony by herself all over the place every day. Patience became her legs.

If it wasn't for the courage and love that the child had for horses, and the patience and understanding that the mare had for that little girl, I never would have accomplished this challenge. God bless ponies everywhere!

Only you can put obstacles in your way when it comes to realizing your dreams, so never say never! The dream continues for me . . .

Sandra L. Costa, Country Star Farm

Biography - "I bought and trained my first horse at 17, a registered Paint pony. While other high school kids were getting cars and making plans for college, I was barrel racing and competing in gymkhanas at local shows. I had aspirations of having my own ranch and training horses and ponies. I moved to Texas in 1981 and have a small farm with 30+ Miniature horses and Shetland ponies. I specialize in breeding Overo Shetlands and Miniature horses. I do all the training and showing of my ponies. I compete in all the state shows in Texas and then travel to the AMHR Nationals, the Shetland Congress and the Pinto World. I have some of the top ponies in the state, winning such titles as AMHR National Top 10, (three of my ponies are in the Miniature Horse Registry Hall of Fame for halter and performance), Pinto World Champion Miniature "B" Division and Shetland Congress Champions."

The Great Spirit Horse

We raise, train and breed Missouri Fox Trotters. I have a mare I have owned for nine years and she has given us several nice colts. Her name is Niangua's Flashdance. One of her colts was fathered by our stallion at the time, Florida's Dancing Fox. We named that foal Niangua's Carousel Dancer. Niangua is a black and white Tobiano, and Carousel is a brown and white Tobiano. Never had the stallion or my mare produced a brown and white Tobiano nor one with blue eyes, but needless to say, Carousel was born with blue eyes and is a brown and white Tobiano.

I have a Lakota Sioux friend named Linda Little Wolf, who is a lecturer on the Plains Indian history. She fell in love with Carousel when he was born and explained to me that he was a "Spirit Horse." Her ancestors believe that blue-eyed, spotted horses are spiritual animals and that they possess supernatural powers. I believed this to be just Indian folklore.

Seven days after he was born, we had to put his father down. I told Linda the sad news and she told us not worry and explained that we have a very precious gift sent from the spirit world. She said, "Carousel was born to bring magic into our lives, to restore balance and harmony to our world." I said, "Oh yeah Linda, another Indian story."

Well, one day last summer, my husband and I had planned to go on a trail ride and I had bathed both horses and turned them into the yard to let them graze while they dried. I was home alone and went into the house to fix some lunch. Before heading in, I closed up everything so they wouldn't get into any trouble while I was in the house. After lunch they looked pretty content out there, so I laid down on the couch and fell asleep.

Much to my surprise, I woke up to this horrible screaming from a horse. I jumped up off the couch to find Carousel standing on my back porch screaming; I couldn't get him off of the step. I finally got the door open and pushed him off the steps - he then proceeded to pick up a planter pot with his teeth and threw it across the yard.

It finally dawned on me - where was my mare, his mother? I ran to the garage and my mare was in there, eating her way through a bag of rye grass seed. As I put the lead rope on her and was walking out of the garage, Carousel came running from the side of the house, reared straight up; shrieked again; ran over; bit his mother on the butt and walked with me down to the barn. My mare was fine, as she had not eaten very much seed, but had this horse not warned me something was wrong, she would have been a very sick animal.

I told my friend about her "Great Spirit Horse." She wasn't surprised and told me how special he was and why he had been sent to us. Horses rarely leave other horses when they are grazing and this colt's mother was nowhere in sight. How did he know I was in the back of the house? He couldn't see inside. It would have been more normal for him to have stayed with her and shared the rye grass seed.

This remarkable horse has been successfully trained by my husband, Don Hart and Chris Martin of our ranch for Linda Little Wolf. He will accompany her to major horse shows all around the country, becoming a vital part of her seminars about Plains Indian folklore and introduced into the show business world as "Wakawacipi." In Linda's native tongue of Lakota, this translates into "Spirit Dancer." Carousel will also be showing in exhibitions all over the United States with Chris Martin, showing the versatility and great disposition of the Missouri Fox Trotter as he dances into the hearts of everyone he meets.

I am now a believer in the legend of the "Great Spirit Horse" and feel privileged to have raised and owned such a wonderful animal.

Sandy Hart of Dancing Fox Ranch

Biography - Sandy Hart and her husband, Don, own Dancing Fox Ranch in Ocala, Florida, 352-236-4399, e-mail shartfox@cs.com. Together they raise, train and show Missouri Fox Trotters. These are gaited horses from the Ozarks of Missouri. Currently, they are standing a stallion that is related to "The Great Spirit Horse" and his name is DM's Never Ending Imprinter. He is a black and white Tobiano, homozygous blue-papered stallion - a sports model with a Cadillac ride. You can visit Sandy Hart at http://www.foxtrottercolor.com/dancingfoxranch

"Wisdom begins in wonder."

Socrates

Cowgirl Dreams do Come True

I have loved horses all my life. I really don't know a life without them, from the days of pony rides at the circus and the long hours spent playing with My Little Ponies, to my current hectic competition and training schedule. I have never grown tired of them or ever questioned my motives.

At a very young age, I was introduced to the world of competition. I have loved the show ring ever since. There is just no way to describe it; the feeling is just like no other. But, as with every other sport, there can be limitations.

I came to realize at a very young age that the horse industry could be very competitive and demanding. I won my first state championship at age ten, my most recent at age sixteen. The winning is awesome, but the best part is the struggle and obstacles that I conquer on my way to the top. Everyone said when I reached middle school my interests would change and riding horses would become part of my past. But my passion only grew stronger and I became more and more determined. I am a junior at a small northeastern Georgia High School where I am a student during the week and a fierce barrel racer and horse show competitor on the weekend.

My latest project is a four-year-old gelding I call Pride, a registered Quarter horse that my parents bought for me as a yearling. His purpose was to be a horse that I could train and make into something through hard work.

When I first got him, he was very spooky and never really acted like he understood what I wanted out of him. He was like this for about two weeks. Slowly, he began to come around and listen to me. I started him really slowly and learned to "read" him.

I rode him in his first show the day he turned three. His first run was really good, but he bucked me off on his second run. Somehow, his attention escaped me and he spooked. I landed *on top* of the second barrel. When I looked up from my fall, he was standing over me with his ears pricked, so I couldn't be mad. I got back in the saddle and took him through the pattern and then dismounted. That incident was his way of telling me to give him time.

As a result, I dedicated the rest of that year to maturing him by exposing him to different things. I took him to clinics and trail rides, and even hauled him to a couple of the shows in which I was currently riding my mare. I would ride him in the warm-up with other horses and then tie him to the trailer and let him learn to trust me and the things I exposed him to. Slowly, he began to have more faith in me.

Before I knew it, a year had passed and it was spring again. My once nervous horse had grown into a smart, mentally and physically tough athlete. I rode him in a few open barrel races that spring and he had improved remarkably. We now had the secret ingredient that wasn't quite there a year ago. We had trust.

I entered him in the state 4-H horse show that summer, as I thought it would be a good experience for both of us. I was not expecting anything record-breaking - I just wanted my horse to listen and trust me. I entered the cone weave, pole bending class, the stake race and barrel race. We had only competed in the cones, poles and stake race once prior to this event, but I shoved this out of my mind. He was also one of the youngest horses at the show, but again, I told myself to "cowgirl up" and ride on faith. I painted a small white cross on each of his shoulders for good luck. We easily made the finals in each class.

In the finals, I made the decision to try for the state championship. We rode the race of our lives. We performed as one. My mom said she saw a look in my eyes she hadn't seen in a long time. We had done the impossible and were crowned the 2000 state champions. This is an instance where the race was not won by speed, but by the power of trust. We won on heart. The prizes were great, but the best part was that I had earned his trust. I asked him to follow my path and he did. I believe he wanted it as much as I did. After years of patience, work, caring and dedication, I had earned the trust of my half-ton partner.

Since that hot June day, the trust we have in each other has grown stronger and stronger. He is my best friend. Currently, we are speeding through barrel patterns all across the southeast. We never doubt each other and our trust in each other has never been shaken.

I have always heard that you are lucky if you come across "one of the great ones" in your lifetime. I believe I already have. Pride is only four, but he has the makings of a legend. Thanks to him I have a happier life and I have experienced the old saying "good things are worth waiting for."

Now before I ride at major shows, I always put a small white cross on each of Pride's shoulders for good luck. If anything can be learned by this story, I hope it is that people can accept that dreams usually don't happen overnight and with love, faith and trust, anything is possible. So never under estimate yourself, because *cowgirl dreams do come true!*

Krystal Mincey

Biography - "I am 17-years-old and live in a small North Georgia community called Dewy Rose. I live with my parents and they are very supportive of me and my busy schedule. I have pretty well been riding and showing horses all my life. I plan on attending UGA and have a goal of becoming an equine veterinarian. My ultimate dream is to win a National Finals Rodeo Barrel Racing World Championship and a AQHA World Congress Pole bending Championship. But as long as my life is with horses, I will be in heaven."

4ᵗʰ Of July Surprise

The fourth of July brought more than picnics, rodeos and fireworks for John Thomas and his family in Colorado; they were blessed with the miracle of twin mules!

Last summer, John came down with a mild case of mule fever and decided to breed his red-roan, Half-Arabian mare, Missy, to Little Jack Horner here at the Lucky Three Ranch in Loveland. The breeding went smoothly and the mare was sent home. She returned in fifteen days for her ultrasound pregnancy check, at which time we learned she had conceived twins. Since the twins posed a life-threatening situation, Kent Knebel, the attending veterinarian, and I advised John of his options: we could abort one and hope the other survived, or we could take the risk and let nature run its course. John opted for the latter and took Missy home. She would be due to foal in August.

In early June, I heard from John again. Missy was enlarging rapidly and John was concerned about her welfare. She was on pasture and could not be watched closely. We agreed that she should return to the Lucky Three Ranch for foaling, where she could be monitored more carefully. In mid-June, Missy returned to the ranch. She was positively enormous… bearing quite a resemblance to a rhinoceros! It was inconceivable that she could carry full term.

A pre-partum vet check revealed some doubt about there still being twins; Kent checked Missy and was only able to feel one baby inside. He said there was a possibility that one of the twins may have been absorbed, or he was very small and hidden beneath the other.

Otherwise, the mare's condition was excellent, and there was nothing to do but wait.

In two weeks, Missy dropped some of her weight and began to look more like a pregnant mare again. Apparently, the pasturing had allowed her to become somewhat obese. She began to wax after two weeks and we were ready for action, but she fooled us. The waxing stage came and went and she began streaming milk wherever she walked. On July 3, Dr. Knebel took another look at her while he was out at the ranch tending to another patient. "Looks like a firecracker birth to me," he announced, "or maybe the day after."

Every hour on the hour, we checked throughout the night. Then, at the 4:00 a.m. check, I was greeted by two darling new faces, one jet black and the other dark bay…the twins had arrived. They were fine, one only slightly smaller than the other; no injury or signs of strain on the mare; and the placenta was intact. I treated the twins' umbilical cords, saw to it that they nursed, then gave them both enemas to assure that the meconium was passed.

It seems in Missy's case, we had all the right things going for us. She was an aged broodmare, able to accommodate the twins. Because the twins are mules, they are stronger and better equipped to grow on less nourishment than are horse babies. They were also born smaller, so their chances of manipulating into position for birth were better. And lastly, both of Missy's foals were females, the stronger of the two sexes.

A proud mother watched carefully as a multitude of visitors came to view the result of this miraculous birth on the fourth of July. Conceived on his birthday and born on the fourth, the twins gave John a good dose of mule fever! He decided to breed Missy again this year, though he felt one baby would be sufficient next time. Little Jack Horner's bray could be heard for miles…the sound of a very proud father!

Meredith Hodges

Biography - Meredith Hodges is one of the most respected people in the Mule industry. Born in Minneapolis and raised in California, Meredith has been associated with mules and donkeys for the past 25 years. She has worked with horses all of her life. Author of the books Training Mules and Donkeys: A Logical Approach to Longears, Training Without Resistance and Donkey Training. She has developed a detailed, step-by-step training series on video that was abbreviated for television and has aired on Outdoor Life Network, the Discovery Channel and HorseTV. She is currently working on a half hour animated TV show for children called, "JASPER" (the mule). Meredith's techniques really work! You can visit Meredith at www.LuckyThreeRanch.com or at www.Willman.com/muletrainer. You can e-mail Meredith at lucky3@willman.com or call 1-800-816-7566. Tours of the Lucky Three Ranch, located in Loveland Colorado, can be arranged by calling 970-663-0066.

The Great Christmas Tree Fiasco

Many years ago - about 4 B.C. (Before Children), to be exact - my husband and I had a Big Adventure. We are no longer married, but that's another story that (hopefully) has nothing to do with this unfortunate incident.

After years of city living, we had just purchased our first home in the country, a run-down cottage in the middle of a swamp on a dead-end road. The basement was constantly under water (we cheerfully called it our indoor swimming pool), the septic system was always backing up and the mosquitoes were so ravenous that we could have benefited from regular blood transfusions. We were often without power, got snowed in every winter, and the roof leaked. But the place was ours, and it was heaven.

To satisfy a life-long dream, we bought a couple of horses to complete the picture. Now, knowing very little about horses at the time, we just scooped up the first likely prospects that came along. Luckily, my little black gelding, Buck, was trustworthy and quiet most of the time. His only major flaw was that he was an escape artist. There was not a stall latch designed that could keep him in.

There was, of course, the unfortunate incident when Buck let himself and his barn mates out one night, then proceeded to the neighbour's stable to release all their horses as well. The police informed us in the morning that the small herd of hoodlums had been terrorizing the surrounding farms and frightening motorists all night long. They implied that "that black one" appeared to be

22

the ringleader. It was all very embarrassing - much like the authorities showing up at your door to tell you that your teenage son had been caught joyriding in a stolen car.

My husband Frank's horse was the complete opposite of Buck. Dubbed Ahab the Arab, he possessed every vice known to the equine world. He hated to be caught, brushed, saddled, bridled and ridden. He tried to kill the vet on several occasions. He refused to pick up his feet to be picked out. He rolled his eyes and spooked at everything on the trail. In short, he was totally neurotic.

Nevertheless, for our first Christmas in the country, we decided it would be oh so romantic to ride off into the bush one moonlit winter night and cut down our own Christmas tree. We saddled up and moved off down the deserted road and into the forest, with the moon casting dark shadows on the blue-tinted snow and the horses' breath suspended in the frosty air.

Deep into the forest, we found a lovely, full spruce and Frank set about cutting it down. As he rode western, it was agreed that he would tie the tree via a long rope to the saddle horn and drag it home - just like the pioneers did.

At least, that was the *plan*.

As we moved off towards home, Ahab rolled his eyes and stared at disbelief and horror at the Giant Tree Monster dragging behind him. The faster he went, the faster the tree went, shushing and cracking over the snowy ground. This was obviously more than his pea-brain could handle, and he just snapped. It was not a pretty sight. Within seconds, he was bolting flat-out through the trees, with Frank cursing and hauling uselessly on the reins. As they were swallowed up by the darkness, I heard a thud, a single strangled cry . . . then silence. I was alone.

Buck, in the meantime, was extremely unhappy that his friend had so rudely departed back to the stable without him, and was digging holes in the snow at a stationary gallop. We headed back at a barely controlled pace, and shortly came across Frank lying face up on the trail, close lined by a low-hanging branch. Together we walked home, being dragged by a frantic Buck, following a trail of pine needles and spruce branches.

Back at the stable, Ahab was waiting. Steam rose from his sweaty flanks, and his sides heaved after his exertions. Miraculously, he was unhurt and the rope was still attached to the saddle horn. At the end of the rope was . . . a stick.

It took us over an hour to cool the horses out. My husband had lost his glasses in the fray, and torn his good coat. We figure the entire caper had set us back well over $200.

The following morning, I meekly drove to the local grocery store and forked over $10 for a tree. To this day, whenever I see a charming Christmas card featuring happy folks dragging home their chosen tree, I still get a little twinge of nostalgia.

But trust me, it quickly passes.

Susan Stafford

Biography - Susan has been the editor of Horsepower Magazine for Young Horse Lovers since its inception in 1988 (www.horse-canada.com). She has owned a variety of equines - from ponies to racing thoroughbreds to a Trakehner stallion - but is currently (and hopefully temporarily) horse-less due to the time constraints of her numerous jobs. She has three children and lives on a small acreage north of Toronto, Ontario Canada.

The Intelligence of the Horse
Chapter Two

For Every Backyard Horse

We called her "Baymare", because that is what she was. At first, it was "Baby-mare", as there wasn't much reason to use her *fancy* name, Beaucoup.

It is true that Baymare came from good stock. She had a famous half-brother that was nine-time conformation champion at "The Garden," but we couldn't afford to show or hunt. We didn't even have a truck or trailer. On the occasions we took her off the farm, it was on her feet.

Over the years, she taught me many lessons - something every horse will do if given half a chance. But since she was the first foal I had ever raised, these lessons were especially important.

Not all the lessons we learn from our trusted equine companions are welcome lessons. Perhaps the most practical thing she taught me was to *always* wear your hard hat. I had grown up in the '40s and '50s, when many newspaper photos showed folks jumping at shows with flying curls or soft fedoras. "Hard" hats weren't even very hard.

One day, I slipped a leg over the old lady, bareback and, as usual, without a hard hat. We took a tour of the lower field. Our little stream had become a haven for beavers. Thinking they now owned the place, they gave us a fair warning with their tails. *SMACK!*

25

Although I have had many a tumble over the years, this one left quite an impression. I can still see the stars! Ever since, I always wear a hard hat, however innocuous the ride may seem.

Another lesson Baymare shared with me during our years together proved to me the intelligence of the horse. This important principle should be understood by any person connected with animals if they are to really understand their partner. One day, I came home and sought out my mare to take a ride before dark. When I finally did locate her, she wouldn't let me get close to her. Expletives were beginning to form on the back of my tongue, when I finally realized that she was trying to lead me somewhere. She would move off, then pause and look back to see if I was following. She led me to our old pony, who was down and dying. I was the one to tell, and she told me as plainly as if she had spoken the words.

Last year, we lost our grand dame. She would have been 33 if she had made it to March 11th. Maybe she wasn't a show champion, but she was a champion around our place. Her fancy name was "Beaucoup" which means "very much" in French - and in our hearts, she was very much indeed.

Elizabeth C. Gathright

Biography - Elizabeth Gathright. "My riding background has been constant since the age of eight, when the Army retired their horses and I got one of them. In my teen years, I hunted with Rockbridge and Fairfax Hunts. Now I am hunting with Oak Ridge. I have shown, but not extensively, and now prefer hunter paces, "light" polo and elementary dressage. Professionally, I am an ASCP registered medical technologist currently working for Georgetown Veterinary and Equine Hospitals in Charlottesville, Virginia."

Tough Guy

He wanted to be a tough guy, but he'd been boarded at a barn with an indoor arena and was seldom ridden outside in inclement weather.

He wanted to be a tough guy, but he was only turned out a couple of hours during the week, weather permitting.

He wanted to be a tough guy, but he constantly wore a blanket that defeated his chances of facing the elements on his own terms.

He arrived in a two-horse trailer, wrapped in his blanket - a victim of a barn management change, in line for a stall at an indoor facility, and in need of an interim home.

He was only here for a month. There was no point in introducing him to the herd in the larger paddock, so he was put with the smaller group.

These guys are "real" horses. They occupy stalls that have 24-hour access to turnout. They wear no blankets. Although each stall has dutch doors, they are seldom closed, and then only in the most severe weather. Horses seem to prefer this arrangement, appear to value the choice, and instinctively select the proper one when it comes to their own well being.

He stood outside in the cold air, trembling in his short coat and refusing to leave his new friends to seek shelter inside. He treasured his new-found freedom. When it was time to leave, he refused to go. His owner tried unsuccessfully to get him to load - and tried again the following weekend, with recruits in tow. Even blindfolding failed to convince him to leave.

I bought him that day, so that he could stay.

That was almost four years ago. He has loaded like a charm ever since – he knows he's coming back. He does not wear his blanket now. His coat grows long and thick in winter. He is a big, strong, powerful boy, living the natural life as much as is possible here in eastern Massachusetts.

He wanted to be a tough guy – and now he is.

Laine Raia

Biography - After 30 years in the corporate world, Laine Raia is the proprietor of "The Ponderaia", a boarding/leasing facility in North Reading, Massachusetts. The Ponderaia, a take-off of the old Ponderosa TV cowboy show, focuses on the mature rider filling a local need as many barns in the area have extensive riding programs geared to children and teenage riders. An English rider and licensed instructor, Laine has ridden out after wild horses on BLM land in both California and Wyoming. A multiple horse owner, Laine also enjoys tacking up Western for a gallop on a nearby beach.

Andalusian Mare

We have a stud farm in New Zealand, where we breed Andalusians. It is the largest pure Spanish breeding farm in New Zealand, and we breed for intelligence, talent and beauty. We are located in the north part of the North Island, and our mild climate allows horses to live outside all year round.

These horses constantly amaze me with their nobility, kindness and spirituality. This story is not one of human/horse interaction, but of horse-to-horse interaction. Having watched the saga unfold in front of my eyes, I have never been able to look at the non-human members of the animal kingdom in the same way.

We had three mares (two pure Spanish Andalusians and one Thoroughbred) with foals at foot, grazing in a five-acre paddock near our house. The paddock had a gully running through the middle of it. The Thoroughbred mare had her part-Andalusian foal, Talisman, sleeping down in the gully, when she decided it was time for tea and wended her way up the hill to stand at the fenceline and beg for a tidbit or two. (We always have lots of grass, but they like a bit of hard feed as a treat for dessert!) The other two mares and foals were standing on the far hill, with their foals sleeping peacefully at their feet.

Suddenly, Talisman awoke. Where was his mum? He couldn't see her, as she was just over the rise of the hill. He called for her. She took not the slightest bit of notice of him, being too far away to hear properly and too busy thinking of her stomach and the possibility of a feed in the offing. He called again. No answer. Panic was setting in, and he was becoming quite distressed, running and calling.

29

I was about to catch the mare and lead her back down to her frightened foal when a wonderful thing happened. The old matriarch, Malana, a noble Andalusian mare, was watching all this from her spot on the rise. She could see the other mare on the hill far away, with Talisman in the dip between them both. She walked to the third mare a few steps away, and I am convinced she asked her to watch her foal. Leaving her own foal in the care of the other Andalusian, she walked down the hill into the gully and "spoke" to the terrified Talisman. Together, they walked up the next hill, the little foal glued to the side of his savior, to where the errant mother stood. After delivering the lost foal, Malana then calmly walked down the length of the paddock back to her own baby, who slept peacefully through the whole episode.

Not only did this event show the caring side of horses - their gentle, mothering instincts - but also the intelligence and thoughtfulness that led the mare Malana to leave her own foal to come to the aid of a frightened youngster.

No one will ever convince me that horses are not intelligent.

Susan Grindell

Biography - Susan Grindell of Bluespur Andalusians is the largest and most successful breeding farm of pure Spanish Andalusians in New Zealand. Our horses combine some of the most prestigious bloodlines from Spain and we have produced countless National Champions, as well as successful competitors in open competition. We have focussed our breeding to enhance the breed's natural beauty and outstanding temperament and have combined this with athleticism and movement for competition. The success of the breeding program is reflected in a high demand for our horses, stretching from New Zealand to the United States." Contact Susan Grindell 64 9 415 8187. Email grins@ihug.co.nz Web site: http://homepages.ihug.co.nz/~grins

Suffering For Our Mistakes

In all the years of living with my Morgan stallion, "Moro Hills Maverick" or Maverick as we called him, there is one experience that taught me more than anything just how attuned to people he is. Years ago, when my daughter, Seanya, was little, we both went out to the field to visit the horses. Seanya went over to Maverick, who was in a stand of trees at the corner of the fenceline.

They were both sharing a quiet moment together when all hell broke loose. Seanya's mare, Revelation, perhaps out of jealousy, came barreling down on Seanya and Maverick, trapping them both in the corner of the field. Revelation turned and started firing away at Maverick with a vengeance with both hind feet. Seanya was directly in front of him, blocking his only escape route. Frozen and caught off guard by the intensity of Revelation's fit of jealous rage, I thought for sure Maverick would run Seanya over. Seanya was frozen in place by Revelation's uncharacteristic display of possessiveness.

After what seemed an eternity, my brain started functioning again and I realized Maverick was taking a beating from Revelation, refusing to run over Seanya in order to save his own hide. I yelled for Seanya to move, so that Maverick could get out of there. Thinking back on it now, knowing that all is well with the three parties involved, the picture in my mind is somewhat funny. I still see my little girl running as fast as her small child's legs could carry her, with a stallion's head above her head, his chest vertically parallel to her back, and his front feet matching her speed and length of stride exactly, never once stepping on her heels or tripping her up. His front feet were taking short, rapid steps, while his hind legs were tucked

31

underneath so far that at any moment I expected to see him sitting on the ground. Revelation was pounding away at his tucked butt - *smack, smack, smack* in rapid succession - like the sound of a butcher's tenderizer mallet hitting a thick piece of steak.

The instant Seanya was out of the trees and he had room to get past her, Maverick made his move for safety. Revelation stopped just as soon as Maverick was away from her "person" and calmly went over to Seanya for attention. To my surprise, Seanya began yelling at Revelation, letting her know that what she had done was wrong.

The mare calmly accepted the tirade, but I don't think it made much of an impact. Seanya was her person and that's all that has ever mattered. As Seanya was venting her fright and anger at Revelation, I sent a long and heartfelt thank-you prayer to Chet and Barbara Treftc of Morrow Hill Morgans for breeding such wonderful horses.

I inspected Maverick to see just how much damage had been done. He jumped when I touched the welts rising on his hindquarters. Thank goodness Revelation had not been wearing hind shoes. None of Revelation's kicks had connected below his gaskins, due to his quick thinking about tucking in his hind end. He had no cuts either. My mother, Seanya and I rubbed him down for a very long time, hoping to lessen the soreness he would soon be feeling and also as a way of saying thank-you for watching out for Seanya. The next day, he was a little stiff, but thankfully got progressively better each day.

Seanya emerged from the experience unhurt, but with a slightly revised opinion of Revelation. To realize that her mare had the capability to be so vicious hurt Seanya a little. I tried to lessen the hurt by explaining that Revelation did it out of jealousy, and only because Seanya had been paying attention to Maverick.

I became aware of the dangers of the infamous "fence corner". All the tales I had heard from other horsepeople and the bad experiences these corners can bring about became real lessons to be remembered. The fact that an innocent animal put a human being above his own safety is a steep price to pay, when it was our fault for being careless in the first place. The stupidity of our mistake has never lessened, but we try to repay Maverick for his endeavors by never repeating our mistakes twice. Because of him, we grow, learn and strive to be the equal of his wisdom and gentleness.

Pamela Michella

Biography - Pamela Michella is 44-years-old and has been with horses since age 7. She has been happily "owned" by Lippitt Morgans since she first met Maverick's sire, Moro Hills Manito, 15-years-ago. For more information about Maverick and his Lippitt Morgan bloodlines, visit him at: http://www.anglefire.com/ny4/lippittmorgans/ If you are interested in owning one of these awesome Lippitt Morgans, you are welcome to visit: http://www.lippittmorgans.com/

Clifford Goes To Camp
(Excerpt From, "Clifford of Drummond Island", by Nancy J. Bailey)

My folks were planning a big shindig on Drummond Island to celebrate 50 years of matrimony. It was the first time in 13 years that all eight of us siblings were going to be together, and I wanted to make the best of it. I was planning to take the horses along, in hopes of talking someone into going riding with me. After all, who could resist an October trail ride through the woods and along the rocky shores of Drummond Island?

My brother, Ted, had arrived from Phoenix and was going to take the six-hour trek north with us for the reunion. I gave Clifford and Trudy, my Morgans, a bath the day before departure, and then covered them with sheets so they would stay clean. Ted was helping me load stuff the next morning. He had some experience with horses, having spent a little time with my sister Raechel's endurance Arabians. He watched while I led Clifford out of the barn, and turned him loose in the yard to graze. "You should have seen Raechel's horse!" Ted said. "When she came to do that endurance ride in Arizona, she brought her horse with her and put it in her back yard. It was bucking and racing around the yard! It was so cute." He was giggling at the memory. I grinned. "Yeah, they sure do like to play sometimes."

We got the trailer hitched and the tack loaded, and then I went into the barn to get Trudy. I led her out, and, like the perfect lady she was, she stepped right into the trailer. Clifford eyed us the whole time. I expected him to follow her, but to my surprise, he suddenly flung his head, gave a squeal, and shot, stiff-legged, straight into the air. He

34

took off galloping, and disappeared around the corner of the house. The dogs followed him in hot pursuit.

Ted watched as Clifford came running by, full tilt, and then disappeared around the corner again. "What is he doing?" he asked. "Just playing," I answered. "Just like we were talking about." I dumped a little grain into the trailer for Trudy, as Clifford made another pass. He woofed as he went by me. I stepped out in his path and waited as he came around the corner again. I pulled a peppermint out of my pocket. "Come here." He trotted up to me, but jigged impatiently while I unwrapped the candy, and then took off again without waiting to take it. He kicked up his heels, squealed and disappeared again behind the house. The dogs followed him joyfully.

Suddenly, it hit me. He was going north! He knew he was going to the north woods, to see Grandpa and have pancakes and trail rides, and have lots of nieces and nephews to hug and kiss him, and show off his tricks! The ritual was always the same: the bath the day before, the sheets, then spending the night in the stall. Then the next morning, off into the trailer they went. He was behaving just like a big happy dog, eager for a car trip.

I started laughing and couldn't stop. If ever an animal was expressing pure joy, it was that horse. Squealing, neighing, jumping and bucking - and he could not settle down enough to even take the candy. I could do nothing but stand there and let him make three or four more circles around the house. He finally skidded to a stop in front of me, blowing, and allowed me to clip the lead rope on his halter. I led him to the open trailer door, and he literally jumped in.

"Wow," Ted said. "He sure isn't like Raechel's horses!"

Nancy J. Bailey

Biography - Originally from Michigan's beautiful Upper Peninsula, Nancy J. Bailey is an author and wildlife artist. She has lived in Alaska, Arizona and Colorado, and currently resides in Michigan with various animals. Nancy is an avid clicker trainer, teaching tricks to dogs, cats, horses and even a goat. "Animals are my best pals. They really have no choice in the matter," she says. She indulges her quirky social habits through community theatre. The book about her equally quirky Morgan gelding, "Clifford of Drummond Island" is available through iUniverse at 1-877-823-9235, or at iUniverse.com. Nancy's artwork can be viewed on line at www.ismi.net/~foxbrush/ArtStudio.htm.

Stinky

I decided to take my Anglo-Arab yearling, better known around the barn as Stinky, to have him considered for the nominated division of the American Warmblood Society inspection. This division is for horses either 100 percent hot blooded or full draft and Stinky is double whammied. After all, the AWS has some nice competition awards and hopefully, in the future, they will be within our reach.

My husband Kim, my son Clint and sister Monica loaded up Stinky and Nasty, Kim's three-year-old filly, and headed to Orlando. After paying all the tolls on the interstate, I was worried I'd have to hock my horse, truck and trailer just to get back home again, but we made it.

It was a beautiful day. There was a wonderful brunch set up and the people were friendly. Kim and Clint were happily hanging out in our new trailer, and Monica was acting as slave for me. Stinky was being a very good boy while we practiced walking and trotting the triangle and standing for the examination. Kim was even so "uncheesy" that he ponied Stinky around on Nasty for a while to loosen him up before the inspection started.

I was busy getting ready; I changed out of my gnarly jeans and put on a nice shirt and slacks with my tennis shoes. At the very least, you want to look like you know what you are doing. This was mistake number one. Monica french-braided my hair (I always wear a baseball cap) and this was mistake number two.

Finally, it was time to start the inspection and I was confident Stinky would be good.

The officials called us to get ready and enter the ring one at a time. Not being one to waste time, I got Stinky in there right away. As soon as we cleared the entry gate - the point of no return - I got a really sick feeling. I began thinking things like, "Oh, my bladder is whining, I have to go to the bathroom!", or "someone else go first, I forgot my whip". What I didn't think of was how incredibly long it always takes the first horse to go.

The inspection started; examining what traits are ideal, strengths, weaknesses, qualities, temperament and movement; My positive thoughts were rapidly disintegrating, as Stinky was getting *really* bored. He was playfully nipping - actually, I was being eaten alive - pawing and wiggling. Then, to top it all off, I heard a tremendously hearty roar of laughter coming from the sidelines. In typical cowboy fashion, my husband yells, "Hey Mona! Look! Did your little horse grow another leg??" Much to my horror, he had, and was happily amusing himself as I stood in disbelief.

I gave the judge a pleading look and we both laughed (I'm glad she had a sense of humor). She said something to the effect of, "If you have a dressage whip. . ." I told her I did and a very kind and sympathetic woman brought it to me. (Not Monica; she was busy videotaping.)

Well, Stinky instantly got a bit better, and reverted back into a four-legged horse, but was still really bored. When we were finally asked to walk on the triangle, Stinky was really moving out. Then he saw Nasty over by the gate and wanted to go say hello. We got back on track after I gave Kim a very nasty look.

Now it was time for the trot. Stinky thought it was post time. The footing was not all that great, but I did my best to keep up. We managed to walk and trot and got a fair score in spite of all the time it took.

I was told Stinky "needed some direction." What I *wanted* to do to him bordered on animal abuse. I wish they could have observed him *after* he left the arena. Stinky was so nice, and we even practiced again just to make sure he was not mentally challenged and if he behaved like a butt rash, to show him I didn't appreciate what he did to me.

Nope, he was perfect. As I walked him back to the trailer, Clint saw me and had to tell me what he thought; "Man, mom, I would have been totally embarrassed!" Thanks baby, was all I could say.

Stinky stood patiently tied to the trailer for two and a half hours while we waited for the event to finish and eat lunch.

When the awards were given, Stinky had managed to get a decent enough score to win the silver medal in the nominated division. All in all, the people were nice, I met some new friends and the food was great. But there are several morals to this story:

Always wear your ball cap on a sunny day, especially if you want to have any brain cells left.

Go ahead and wear your gnarly jeans - you're going to get dirty anyway.

If you have to go to the bathroom, *go.*

Being last in line is not always a bad thing.

Do *not* have your sister videotape anything for you.

And lastly, owning any stud colt and having a cowboy husband might result in the colt having missing body parts the next morning, especially if your husband's knife is sharp and it's that time of year when bull calves become steer calves.

Mona L. Malone

39

Biography - Mona L. Malone. "I am married and have two boys: Justin. 18, and Clint 13. We have four horses, three dogs and three cats. We live on the Anclote River Ranch (3400 acres) located in Odessa, Florida, where my husband Kim is the ranch foreman. The ranch was mainly a commercial cow/calf operation and has now branched out to the eco-tourism industry, where we give guided tours. We are involved in barrel racing, reining, working cow horses, and starting and training our own colts. I thank God for the beauty around me and the gift of writing."

Overcoming Adversity
Chapter Three

Lucky Icicle Blue

In June of 1996, my husband, Jay, purchased a steel-grey three-year-old Quarter Horse gelding named Ice. He was about 14-hands-high and as skinny as a rail. The primary reason why Jay bought Ice was because I said that Ice reminded me a lot of Jack, the horse Jay had just sold. So Ice came home with us that very day. And as Jay put it, he went on the "Hurd" feeding program.

I did most of the work on the ground with Ice, which included feeding time, and working with the vet and farrier. Poor Ice didn't know what happened to him for a while. Ice has all the characteristics of a good using horse and I told Jay that with some work, we would be repaid for our efforts. Ice acted a bit flighty with certain things and based on his behavior, we figured at some point in his young life he had been abused.

Jay worked with Ice for several years and the horse got some experience and confidence under his belt. Then Jay decided to take Ice to a horsemanship/team-penning clinic that a friend was hosting. When Jay returned from the clinic, it was clear that Ice was a natural when it came to team penning but he needed to refine his skills. However, Jay felt that since he trained Dollar, our older gelding, to work with cattle, maybe he could teach Ice, too.

That winter, we set off for a team penning practice at the Diamond 7 arena. There, we found out that Ice had a few more bugs that needed to be worked out. Specifically, he was frightened of indoor riding

41

arenas, especially if they had wall panels. I told Jay I would start working with Ice and see if I could turn him around. I'd done a lot of the "fix-it" training on Dollar, so why not?

My favorite book during the planning of Ice's rehabilitation was "Debugging Your Horse" by Bonnie Marlewski-Probert. I started setting up a step-by-step campaign to overcome Ice's fears. We went to the indoor arena that sported the dreaded panelled walls. Ice had been here the previous year for Bill's team penning clinic. For moral support, we took Dollar. The events on this particular evening were fun events. Ice's first event to tackle was barrel racing; mind you, I'm not a gamer, so this was all new to me. Ice and I went around the first barrel, then he decided it was time to head for home. I told him no and added pressure with my left heel. We ended up doing the barrels a couple of times. Poor Ice had to have Dollar walk him through the alley that night and sometimes through the entrance gate.

The next week, I worked with Ice by himself in a little arena off of the barn. Ice had a trick of locking up and rolling back to his left, so I was prepared and had taken my riding crop out in the arena with me. I held it close to my body, so Ice really was not sure if I had it or not. I was working towards the end of the pen when Ice pulled his trick, but unfortunately for him, I was ready. I was holding the crop and when he spun around, it hit him in the shoulder. My debugging of the situation had worked. Ice ran into the crop with a nice "whack" and he just froze. I told Ice "whoa" and then patted him on the neck. He did not try his trick again.

The next week was the fun show again. Since Ice was spooky about objects near his face, I thought maybe pole bending would do the trick.

Before we went to the event, I consulted with Bonnie and she suggested I have Ice's eyes checked. I did, and the vet discovered that Ice had an iris cyst in his left eye. This completely explained why he would always spin left and why he was so spooky. Now that we understood why Ice had been behaving this way, we worked out a plan to help him overcome his problem. Our vet recommended that we desensitize Ice to movement on that side, so we made the decision to focus on pole bending.

We entered the pole bending for the first time and he took one look at all the poles in their nice row and decided to stay about four feet off them. I started up the arena at a slow trot, which was good enough for me. We started the pattern and Ice was fine. He was a little hesitant about going back through the poles, but he decided that if I asked him to go back, there must be a good reason. It worked. Every time Ice went into the arena, he was more confident of himself and of me. With our newfound success, our next challenge was to try the team penning again.

We returned to the same clinic as the year before and this time we took both horses. Jay of course was a veteran of the clinic, but Ice also had the experience of working in this particular arena during the fun shows. By the end of the clinic, Ice was doing things that Jay could not get him to do the year before.

Now that we have factored his handicap into our training program, Ice has really come around. He is doing new things now that demonstrate his newfound level of confidence in himself and in his caretakers.

When we first got Ice, we could not even clip his whiskers, let alone his ears or bridle path. I've made a special effort to work with Ice on clipping. Every time he would let me clip him - or even touch the clippers to him, especially in the ear or bridle path area - he would get a treat. Now, after a lot of patience and persistence, I can clip him with just a halter and lead rope hanging from his neck. My husband can't believe the changes in Ice and since we have moved to a more relaxed boarding stable, things have only gotten better.

Because we took the time to find out what was really wrong with Ice and have incorporated that handicap into our riding and training each day, nothing much fazes him anymore. He is often braver than horses that have no visual problems at all.

Earlier this year, I had the chance to see if Ice remembered how to work cattle since his experience at the clinic roughly six month earlier. Ice seemed to remember everything!

This little horse that came to us underweight and easily spooked is now eight-years-old. He constantly amazes Jay and I with his courage and confidence by embracing new challenges that we never thought he could face.

Julie Anne Hurd

Biography - Julie Anne Hurd currently resides in York County, Pennsylvania, with her husband Jay and their horses. "I have been horse crazy for as long as I can remember. My parents bought my sister and I Breyer models growing up and provided us with riding lessons for several years. I purchased my first horse at age 19 with the help of my parents. My husband and I share a love of horses and they are a big part of our life together."

Letting Go Of A "Dream"

I can remember the day as if it was yesterday - November 19, 1997. I was sitting in my fourth period English class, bored out of my mind, when I was told that I had an early dismissal. As I drew closer to the office, I saw my mom and dad. They were crying. "What's wrong?" I asked. My parents took me outside, and their words will remain with me forever. "Dream was out in the pasture playing, and she broke her leg. When the vet called our house, we weren't home, so they put her down, rather than let her suffer. They're going to bury her tonight. Do you want to say good-bye?"

My body felt numb, as if a train had hit me. My blood was slowing down, my breath was coming in short gasps, and my eyes flooded with tears.

Dream is - was - my pony. Her show name was "Solitary Dream," and she was a beautiful Quarter Horse, although she was built more like a Thoroughbred. She had long slender legs, and a beautiful tail that gracefully floated as she moved. Dream always had a presence about her that let you know that she *knew* she was special.

Ada, the vet, wasn't Dream's regular vet, but she was returning from taking her daughter to the school bus stop when she saw Dream standing in the front of the pasture with blood covering her leg. Dream had already gone into shock, and was in desperate need of help. Ada ran into the pasture and called the barn manager, Cindy, and a trainer, Melissa. They all decided that her leg was too bad to fix, so after they tried to reach me, they made the decision to put her out of her misery. Everyone knew that I loved Dream and that I would not have wanted her to suffer.

The ride to the barn was grim, and everyone was crying. When we got to the barn, Cindy and Melissa emerged from the depths of the barn's shadows; they were also crying. We went down the driveway to the back field, where Dream was resting. What I saw shocked me worse than a horror show. Her leg was mangled. Her cannon and splint bones were neatly split in half, and all the tendons, ligaments, and muscles were ripped far beyond repair. Her eyes were peacefully shut forever.

Dream was buried that night, and I visited her grave the next week and planted pansies and tulip bulbs. To my despair, rabbits ate the pansies and the frost killed the bulbs. Since then, I've only visited her grave twice; it's still too painful.

There's no possible way to explain how I felt that day. Nothing could have prepared me for that, and it's something that I will never forget. It's so hard to say good-bye to your first pony that way and to know that you will never get to see her again. I just hope that somewhere there's a horse heaven where all horses can meet and spend eternity in the skies doing what they love to do. Hopefully, horse lovers are allowed there as well, and I will one day be reunited with my Dream who left me all too soon.

Melissa Merkle

Biography - Melissa Merkle. "I am currently 15-years-old. I have been riding horses since I was eight, and they are a major part of my life. After Dream passed away, I got a new pony four months later, and now, after four years, I have sadly outgrown him. I now have a horse that I recently bought, and I am planning to do extensive showing with him on all levels. I haven't been able to sell my pony, because I still can't forget how hard it is to let your baby go."

Beauty

Beauty was born in May of 1995. She was the first foal I ever raised and I was there for her conception and birth. I vowed to her that she would never leave or ever be harmed. She would live the life not all horses get to live; one filled with love and devotion.

She was a pretty little bay filly out of the Doc Bar line and I named her Niki's Little Beauty or "Beauty" to us. From day one, she was sweet; loving and eager to please. She loved people and would canter to the fence to meet anyone who came by. I heard nothing but compliments on how she was such a sweet and loving foal at such a young age – never shying away, but wanting to be petted and loved.

We spent many wonderful times together and she was my friend and confidant. Beauty shared her pasture with her mother, Niki, a Buckskin Quarter horse and Uncle Red, my big sorrel Appaloosa. It was common to see her off playing with her Uncle Red, but when mom called, she would run back as the dutiful daughter she was!

Years passed and I kept my word to her. She was a happy and well-adjusted little mare and stayed that way during training. We had a trainer come to our farm so that we could supervise her progress and be assured nothing would ever harm her. Beauty was a quick learner and advanced rapidly. She lived up to her name in both looks and manners.

In the spring of the year she was to turn four, we decided to breed both she and her mother in hopes of starting a small breeding farm. I wanted to see sweet little foals cavorting in beautiful spring grass.

There is nothing more beautiful than horses grazing in a pasture. Actually, I believe that horses are the most beautiful creatures God created.

About this time, my husband decided he wanted a trail riding horse and the search began. We lucked out and found a gorgeous flaxen-maned sorrel Quarter horse. Geronimo quickly became part of the family.

It was springtime in Virginia and Beauty's birthday was only a few days away. One Saturday evening, we had gone to bed and during the night a thunderstorm rolled over us, as they are prone to do during that time of the year.

The next morning, my husband went to the barn and I followed a few moments behind, only to be intercepted by him on my way. He had the monumental task of telling me that Geronimo and Beauty had been killed by lightening. We don't think it was a direct strike, but clearly close enough to kill them instantly.

Even today, two years later, my heart aches over our loss. Losing Geronimo was awful, for we had bonded and he was such a sweet-heart. But my heart's love, my closest friend and ally lay at my feet, never to come when I called or be there for me when I needed someone to tell my secrets to. I couldn't stop crying; life was so unjust. I had promised to take care of her and I had let her down somehow. My only comfort was that it was a quick and merciful end.

Thank goodness our family and friends were there for us. We picked out a beautiful, pastoral place for the horses to be buried and I was asked to leave so I wouldn't have to watch. I cried for weeks and to this day, my heart breaks when I think of Beauty. It is still difficult for me to speak about her. I keep her picture on my wall and her baby picture and first set of shoes. She may be gone, but she lives in my heart. If there is a God, I know she is waiting for me in heaven.

Epilog:"Niki, Beauty's mother, was bred anyway because we had already paid the fees. Sadly, that foal was born too early and died. We rebred her, although I really didn't want to because we had lost so much already, but life goes on and we eagerly await Niki's new foal.

Michele Smith

Biography - Michele Smith. "I live with my husband on our Quarter Horse breeding farm, 5 Springs Farm, in Powhatan, Virginia. I have two grown children and three grandchildren whom I am trying to influence to share my love of horses. I have been around horses most of my life and am just realizing my childhood dream to breed horses and to one day in the spring see a pasture filled with mares and foals. There is nothing more beautiful!"

The New Horse

It was definitely his eyes that convinced me to take a chance.

Everyone thought I was crazy, buying an unbroken, highly excitable nine-year-old gelding, especially one who had rarely been handled and had spent the last seven years in a small, muddy paddock with another horse, living life *his* way. His tail had been chewed off, his coat and mane were scraggly, and a large bumpy scar sat prominently on his face from an old nail injury. The only trimming his feet received over the years came from him wearing them down by pacing - which he did a lot.

But his eyes told me something else; deep brown, almond shaped, and trimmed in black that stood out against his golden-colored palomino coat. They said, "Please, I'm really a good horse under all the dirt and grime. I will do anything for you, if only you pay attention to me." It was a plea for a human of his own.

I had seen that look before. It was in the eyes of my two-year-old Appaloosa, (Pink Panther's) Kaito, when I bought him seven years ago. That's when my barrel racing trainer and friend, Lee Northup, convinced me that a green horse and a green rider were not always a bad combination, if you are open to advice, willing to take your time and never, ever lose your temper. She was right - I've never had a more loyal companion. He does everything I ask to the level at which I am capable of riding him - barrels, dressage, trail riding, even overnight camping. And he still whinnies when I walk up to him. I'm convinced he would lay down his life for me. Now he performs his most important job ever - he is teaching my daughter. But would it be the same with this one? Santana. His name conjured up images of the hot and strong California wind, as well as the spectacular comeback of the rock guitarist - a question of talent and timing. He would definitely challenge my horsemanship skills and patience. He was pushy, but then he had never been told "no." He had experienced nothing, but was curious, smart and full of energy. In my view, there was a lot of potential and he was worth the effort. I convinced his skeptical owner that he was worth selling, with the agreement that if it didn't work out, he would be returned. So on Christmas Day, 1998, Santana came to live in our barn, red ribbon and all.

I knew his training would have to be done in small steps. I learned that from horse trainer John Lyons - when you measure progress in inches, you always move forward. The trick is to break everything down to small enough tasks. For example, teaching him to drop his head by giving to pressure on his poll with my hand only took 10 minutes, but now I had the basics on which I could build. Putting on his halter, brushing his forelock, leading, putting on his bridle, teaching him to give to the bit and relaxing him; all of these are built on that first lesson of giving in to pressure and rewarding it with the release. It also gave me my most valuable tool – teaching him to drop his head (the "calm down" cue) when he got wound up. To those watching, it looked effortless. To me, each small step was hard work, yet rewarding at the same time.

I was also aware that I needed to keep good training notes, because I knew that when I got frustrated (we are human, after all), I would forget how far we had come. Sometimes you have to step back to the previous lesson and reinforce it. That doesn't mean that he "has an attitude," it means he didn't learn the lesson or you didn't teach it well enough and you need to repeat it until he does. Those inches add up to feet and eventually miles. And we have come miles and miles since our first ride two years ago.

We've learned a lot together - Santana's gaits are the smoothest I've ever experienced and his spirit and energy are amazing. It's no longer intimidating, high-strung nervous energy – its been redirected into impulsion. He has such raw talent that he has challenged me to

51

become a better rider. Every mistake I make is immediately obvious, because he is listening to my every move. I have never once felt that I could not control him, even with 1,200 pounds of neurons firing all at once and feeling like an explosion is imminent. And you can't do it with a whip or a chain - it's the trust that has the biggest impact. He knows immediately when he has done something right and he loves the attention. If he does something wrong, I tell him in my most (probably louder than I want to admit) motherly voice, and he's crushed. It's being strict and kind at the same time - day after day after day. Granted, he is not perfect (yet). He is impatient, especially with the farrier - but some things take more time than others.

I had a friend tell me to hire someone who would put Santana in his place and break his spirit. I didn't want his spirit broken. I didn't want a "personality-less horse". It's his spirit that makes him who he is and gives him the drive and motivation to be so dynamic. I'd rather invest the time in training than invest the money in breaking!

My dressage trainer, Bruce Graham, is helping me with Santana's next step - building the muscle strength and suppleness for him to reach his highest level of performance. He also is helping me develop a better seat and to learn gymnastic exercises. As Bruce often says, "There is no limit to what he can do, if you give him the tools to do it with. The notes are all the same - it's how you put them together that creates the music."

If you notice, I have drawn from many disciplines for my training approach: barrel racing, dressage, and basic training techniques. Most of my basic work is done in my Western barrel saddle, and then gets refined with my dressage saddle.

It's amazing how much my various teachers and trainers have in common, even though the *final music score* is very different. But each has added their own piece to the puzzle. Lee taught me to keep the fun in horses. She showed me that not everything had to be "by the book" and that sometimes a good gallop down the beach does wonders for the mind and soul. John Lyons taught me that every interaction with your horse should be positive, but the trick is to keep your expectations realistic. Bruce taught me that a horse is only limited by his rider. A brilliant rider can turn an average horse into a brilliant one!

So maybe you'll see Santana and me at a show this year – just look for the horse with the happy eyes.

Kathleen Monan Castro

Biography - Kathleen Monan Castro is a relative newcomer to horse training, having bought her first horse in 1993. "I am proud that horses are my mirror and reflect the time and patience I have given them - they are as different as night and day." Among those who have been most helpful in her education are Lee Northup, who trains horses for the Rhode Island Providence Mounted Police and competes in barrel racing events. Bruce Graham is the creator of www.edressage.com and continues to teach his students the principle of harmony between horse and rider. John Lyons who is a well-known trainer and author of several books who runs clinics throughout the USA.

A Dream Comin' True

This is a story of a woman and her Morgan filly. It is a story of courage and love, of patience and determination. It is a story of the human spirit and the essence of the Morgan heart. It is a story that I hope will encourage you to reach for the stars and realize your dreams.

Susan Keenan has owned and trained horses for well over 20 years. The breeds that she has owned include Appaloosas, Thoroughbreds, a Half-Arabian and currently a yearling Morgan filly, Black Lake Bewitched, (aka Sparkle). While mainly using her horses for pleasure trail riding, Sue has also enjoyed considerable success in the show ring, most notably with her Half-Arabian mare, Tarifa, who was a many times champion halter mare up and down the East Coast.

What makes this woman so unique and noteworthy is that Sue is afflicted with Hereditary Spastic Paraparesis or HSP, a severe spastisity and weakness of the muscles. HSP is a rare enough disorder and in Sue it is even more rare in that in the majority of HSP patients, the affected muscles are generally in the lower extremities. Sue has the dubious distinction of having it affect her muscles from the neck on down, resulting in tremendous difficulty walking and considerable problems with her balance. This has been a slowly progressive condition, but not one Sue has let interfere with her life, career or her love of horses, although it had prohibited her from ever being able to handle, ride or drive her own horse in a class or competition.

Countless times Sue sat at the rail and watched her horse being shown by others - until now! Enter into the picture one Morgan filly, one electric wheelchair/scooter and one golf cart. Add to the mixture the help of willing and supportive friends and what was created was magic.

Sue has long had contact with the Morgan breed through friends who own Morgans and compete in a variety of disciplines. When she owned and competed her Half-Arabian, she stabled with me. I owned Morgans, as did a lot of our friends stabling there. While Sue was boarding her mare at a private stable in Philadelphia, Pennsylvania., the manager's Morgan mare, Sun South Brittany, foaled a chestnut filly sired by the farm's senior stallion, the many times in-hand and pleasure driving champion, Antietam On Command. It was the proverbial love at first sight when Sue saw the foal. Somehow, she couldn't resist her and in losing her heart to the captivating red filly, the seeds of an idea were sown. A dream long sidelined came to the fore: to one day show this filly - the product of a breed renowned for its willingness, adaptability and versatility - herself. The spellbinding chestnut filly became known as Sparkle, with her registered name aptly being Black Lake Bewitched.

From day one of her life, Sparkle knew Sue and accepted her with all her special trappings; the cane was something to nibble on and to take direction from, the electric scooter was how she accompanied her dam to the paddock. Sparkle learned, without any prompting it seemed, to measure her walk to Sue's halting steps with the cane.

Once weaned, Sparkle graduated to the golf cart and it became a routine occurrence to see Sue ponying the filly around the farm and out on the trails. The filly's generosity and willing nature is such that although she may snort and cavort like any other exuberant youngster, she listens to Sue and has never threatened any harm, even inadvertently. A softly spoken reprimand from Sue, direction with the lead or cane, and Sparkle works alongside or around the golf cart at all gaits and over all types of terrain.

Given the ease with which Sparkle took to the adaptations needed to accommodate Sue's special circumstances, the old dream of showing her own horse was reborn. A local all-breed equestrian club, the Huntingdon Valley Riding and Driving Association, was the pioneer in allowing Sue to show Sparkle. On May 17, 1998, the dream became reality: Sue showed her now yearling Morgan filly to a second in halter mares and a first in grooming and showmanship. The ribbons paled in comparison to the overwhelming joy felt by not only Sue, but by all those fortunate to have witnessed this momentous occasion. When one talks of occasions that uplift the human spirit, this one surely is right up there among the leaders.

In August of 1998, this unique filly and her equally inspiring owner/handler made their "A" level debut at the Mid-Atlantic Regional Championship Morgan Horse Show. Sue capably exhibited Sparkle in the sport horse suitability three years and under class. Walking and trotting the patterns alongside Sue in the golf cart, Sparkle showed like a veteran and came away with not only a ribbon in this, one of the highest percentage-scoring sport horse classes, but also with a perfect 10 for manners!

With such an auspicious beginning, the future looks bright indeed. Sue's goals of training Sparkle to drive and compete in carriage and then to ride and show Western pleasure are certainly within the pair's grasp. Sue has ridden and driven throughout her equestrian career, but her mount must possess great patience and self-control, for it takes her some time to mount and dismount. Sparkle, young as she is, already displays the predilection for these talents. For the time being, though, and as they will throughout their lives together, Sue and Sparkle are enjoying their partnership as they gallivant about the farm and down the trails.

There is an old Cherokee saying that sums it all up quite succinctly: "We can only be what we give ourselves the power to be." More power to you, Sue!

Author's note: Sue achieved another of her goals; in the fall of 2000, she started riding the three-year-old Sparkle, but that is another story…

Overcoming Adversity

MaryAnn Schafer

Biography - MaryAnn Schafer, a Pennsylvania native, became involved with Morgans in 1974. She was drawn to the breed by their versatility, willing attitudes, and love of people and purchased her first Morgan mare, Topfield's Sunrise, in 1977. She now has a daughter and two granddaughters of Sunrise and is committed to continuing the Morgan legacy of versatility thru them. With Sunrise's daughter, Bowood Elusive Dream, she attained what she considers the ultimate partnership. Together, they participated in shows, CDE's, dressage, combined training and competitive trail, culminating in Dream becoming the first mare ever to earn the elite AMHA Sport Horse Award. I encourage people to do lots of different things with their horses, regardless of breed, as it makes it more interesting to all!

Springtime Is My Favorite Time

Springtime is my favorite time of year, although the Tennessee climate is fickle. My husband and I were on foal watch duty beginning the first of March, 2000, and the weather had been unseasonably warm. That is, until we began our nightly vigil in the tack room. We snuggled into sleeping bags and waited for signs of a new baby. Our 11-year-old National Show Horse mare was due around March 10, and although it was a little early to expect an arrival, we didn't want to take any chances. The truth was that we loved to sleep in the barn amid the night sounds of the horses.

Like many middle-aged horse lovers, I had been involved with horses as a child. But with maturity came other responsibilities and horses fell by the wayside. In the early '90s, I came to the realization that I wanted to make more memories by which to grow old, and that raising horses was the way I wanted to spend the rest of my life.

So we moved to Tennessee with our Arabian horses, one of which was Lilli, the beautiful bay mare now due to foal. We built a barn, complete with birthing stall, and set our sights on raising babies. The first filly was born in April of 1997, in a textbook foaling. The second filly was born in 1999 and was truly a miracle. Now, we waited with great anticipation for the third to enter the world.

On the morning of March 15, I noticed that Lilli was pacing the paddock more than usual. Instead of consuming her hay, she only inspected it and walked away. Around 3:00 p.m. I brought Lilli into the birthing stall and wrapped her tail. I then noticed wax on her nipples and a little sweat on her shoulders. I fed her and she ate a complete meal, but this time she snatched at her hay and paced.

At 10:00 p.m. we turned the lights out and my husband went to the house to sleep (by this time the excitement of the nightly vigil had worn off). As soon as the barn was dark, Lilli started pacing and urinating. I watched her in the nightlight from the tack room observation window. She knew I was there, though! She made a point to stop just where I could see her.

By 10:15, I knew that she was going to foal, so I called my husband to come back to the barn. As he was sneaking back inside, Lilli's water broke and she lay down. She immediately stood back up and I noticed that the foal's feet were emerging. They were pointed in the right direction, so we both relaxed. Lilli lay down again and this time she quickly pushed the foal out. We fought the urge to go into the stall; we knew that the best thing to do is let mother and baby bond for a few minutes without interruption. Besides, Lilli is an experienced broodmare and is very good with her foals.

In the dim light we could see that the foal was working its way out of the amnion, and Lilli soon reached around and started to assist. Then the foal sat upright, although weakly. We decided to go in at this point. My husband dried the baby and announced that we had a colt. Although we had heard that colts were harder to handle than fillies, we were so relieved that mother and baby were fine, the gender didn't matter.

The foal finally stood and nursed after two hours, and then only with assistance. I thought that this was a little odd, especially since Lilli had gone beyond her due date, and the colt was very large. But everything else appeared to be progressing normally. Now we waited for daybreak and the vet's checkup.

The vet arrived early in the morning to examine Lilli and the colt, and he pronounced them both fit. He also thought that it was odd that a colt, especially one this big, would take so long to stand and nurse, but he didn't think it was anything to worry about.

In her past pregnancies, Lilli had been very calm throughout and had never minded anyone being near her or the foal. This time, however, she had to be restrained while the vet examined the colt. He told me to watch her and let him know if she didn't settle down.

On the third day, Lilli and the colt were in the paddock getting some fresh air. As I observed them from the barn, I noticed the colt attempting to nurse several times and stopping. He would just dribble the milk to the ground. On further observation, I noticed that Lilli had "bagged up" and was streaming milk continuously. I knew that a healthy foal should keep his dam drained at all times. Something was definitely wrong.

I called the vet. His first thought was that the colt had been too greedy and had overindulged on mother's milk, and that it was not uncommon for colts to do this. He was enroute to another call and said that he would call back within the hour to see how things were going.

In the meantime, I brought Lilli and the colt back into the barn. I noticed that he had watery, greenish diarrhea. I panicked, knowing that a colt can get dehydrated quickly. Without the ability to nurse, this was a dire situation. This baby was in jeopardy. The hour I waited for that vet's call seemed like an eternity. When I updated him on the situation, he said that he was on the way. He told me to blanket the colt while we waited. We hoped for the best, but feared the worst.

As soon as the vet arrived, he went to the colt, which was standing weakly against the wall of the stall, shifting his feet back and forth. He had a dull look in his eyes, where before he was very alert. Initial examination showed no fever. The vet gave him an injection of banamine and started an I.V. to restore fluids to his body.

Lilli was very agitated during the examination and had to be restrained. She seemed easily spooked, which was unlike her. She had always been a calm mother, but we attributed this behavior to her concern for her sick colt. The vet left with instructions for the night and made arrangements to come out the next day. We kept vigil overnight, on pins and needles every time we went to check on the colt. Our worst nightmare was looming over us. What if this newborn didn't make it?

Early the next morning the vet came out to find the colt in the same condition. While the medicine had stabilized him through the night, with the new day we would have to take action immediately if we wanted to save this precious life.

The vet drew blood on both Lilli and the colt; he analyzed it immediately and found nothing irregular, but Lilli was running a slightly elevated temperature. She was given an antibiotic while the vet ran another I.V. for the colt. By this time the colt was not even attempting to nurse. The vet said that we needed to talk.

He sat down with my husband and me and relayed the options: 1. Take the colt and Lilli to a 24-hour facility, in this case University of Tennessee; 2. He would make daily trips out to treat the colt; 3. We could learn what he did when he treated the colt and take responsibility for treatment; or 4. Put the colt down. We knew that the hospital would be very expensive, although it would be the best bet; the bill for the vet would be insurmountable if he made daily trips out; and letting the colt die was not even an outside option. Business-wise, it would have made sense, but neither or us have ever placed business at a higher priority than our hearts.

Before we made the decision, however, we talked with the vet at great length about the costs involved for the other three choices. As the vet walked away to give us a moment to speak privately, the colt struggled to his feet and walked over to Lilli and attempted to nurse. My husband looked at me and said, "we have to save him ourselves. I can take time from work and stay at home to help nurse him back to health. If we don't try, I will never be able to live with myself."

The decision was made. We listened to the vet as he explained and wrote down exactly what needed to be done. Not only did the colt need round-the-clock care, Lilli had an infection that the vet believed had been passed to the colt in utero. This would explain his weakness at birth, the shivering, and most importantly, his distaste for his mother's milk. I have never seen a more pitiful sight than this baby trying to nurse and being unable to.

The first thing that the vet did was pass a tube through the colt's nose. Through this tube we were to administer electrolytes every four hours, Foal Lac milk every four hours and Pepto-Bismol every fours, with the times being staggered so as not to overload his small stomach. We also took his temperature every four hours and he was given hip shots of dmso and banamine nightly. In addition, Lilli had to be temped every four hours and milked twice daily. We were novices in basic equine health care, let alone emergency care. But, I have always heard that in a crisis, you do what you have to do. For 72 hours straight, we both doctored and kept vigil, sometimes drifting off to sleep just in time for the alarm clocks to ring.

It was heartbreaking to watch the colt shiver as he did when the cold liquids went into his stomach; on top of this, the weather had turned cold and rainy. To help alleviate the coldness of the birthing stall, my husband installed a heat lamp in each corner.

We began to notice that the colt appeared to be more bright-eyed, although he still had diarrhea and was not nursing. Each morning, the vet called for a progress report and to give further instructions. After five days of continuous medication, the lack of sleep took its toll on us. We were trying to sneak a nap when I awoke to a loud, unmistakable sound – a nursing slurp! The colt got in two gulps before he walked away. We were so relieved to see this sign of progress. We knew that this was only a minor achievement and that we had a long way to go, but it was the first positive move the colt had made. At this point all tiredness left us, and we spent the rest of the day watching as he nursed several more times. The number of swallows slowly increased and by nighttime he was nursing with almost normal regularity.

While we were encouraged by the colt's improvement, the vet warned of possible stomach ulcers. So much medicine had been pumped into his tiny stomach; he told us to watch him closely for signs of discomfort.

The shots that had been given nightly were discontinued, and we were glad of it. There is no sound so heart-wrenching as a tiny colt whining. With everything the little colt had been through since his entrance into the world, we were afraid that the imprinting would fall by the wayside. We wouldn't have blamed him if he never let a human being touch him again.

By the end of a week, the colt was on his way to recovery, Lilli was physically back to normal, and her laid-back manner of mothering soon returned.

The vet examined Lilli and the colt, which we had now named. We felt that he had to have been touched by an angel, and he was truly a blessing to us. We named him Gabriel's Blessing, and we call him Gaybe.

The vet removed the stomach tube - a major deal for Gaybe, and for us - and said that he felt guardedly optimistic that Gaybe would be all right. The vet also said that a lot of people wouldn't have made the sacrifices we did for a horse, but the fact that we took on the responsibility says a lot for the kind of people we are. For two people who were face-to-face with the loss of a precious life, we both can say that we would do it all over again. We only need to walk to the barn and hear Gaybe call us to know it was well worth it!

Emily Lineberger Bridges

Biography - A North Carolina native, Emily Lineberger Bridges was involved with horses as a child. With adulthood came other responsibilities, but she dreamed of the day when horses could take priority. In 1992, Emily began riding again, and in 1996 she moved with her Arabian horses to Lebanon, Tennessee. With this move came a start-up horse keeping operation, including a family-built barn. She and her husband, Ron, own Summerwind Farm where they raise purebred and Half-Arabian horses with Polish and Crabbet blood-lines. Their primary focus is on breeding and foal development. Emily's description of her life with her horses? "Living the Dream!"

Choose Your Partners Wisely!
Mescalero

I had a farm in Iowa; actually, I rented one. While finishing up my Animal Science degree at Iowa State University, I was fortunate to share a great farm northwest of Ames with three other students.

During that time I usually had two horses - my personal mount, a seasoned grade mare named Mescalero, and another as a training project.

At the time of this story, my second horse was "Mr. Slinky", a Quarter Horse gelding I had just started under saddle. The "under saddle" part is really a misnomer, because I had only ridden him bareback. Mr. Slinky was still very, very green.

So when Jerry, a friend from Des Moines, visited us one weekend and asked to ride, saying he was an experienced rider, I put my prized Western saddle on my good mare, Mesc, and handed him the reins. I figured the length (and success) of our ride would depend on how well Slinky performed for me.

The first part of the ride went smoothly as we moseyed through the walnut, oak and elm and meandered along the Skunk River, crossing it a couple of times where I knew it was safe. I indicated where we should go and when it would be a good time for us to trot. Slinky was gaining some good reining experience, weaving through the timber, and Mescalero was giving Jerry a nice ride. I was pleased.

65

It was when Jerry's testosterone neutralized his common sense that we ran into trouble. At the midpoint of our ride, we were ready to head back to the farmhouse and had to cross the creek one last time.

I called back over my shoulder something like, "It's solid here." Slinky picked his way carefully across a shallow, wide crossing littered with large round stones that made the water roil and burble. I just assumed Jerry and Mesc were behind me.

But Jerry had a more daring crossing in mind, about 50 feet upstream at a bend where the creek ran narrow and deep and dangerously quiet, with a steep dirt bank on the opposite side. I swivelled on Slinky's back just in time to see Mesc obediently wade into the water and head for the cut bank. Her labored movements told me she was dealing with very soft footing, but she was making it across.

I have to digress here for a minute. One thing I have always felt very strongly about is developing and maintaining a horse's trust. Because I never ask my horses to do the obviously unsafe or impossible, my horses trust my judgment. In turn, I entrust them with my safety. With that mutual respect, it is quite amazing what a horse and rider are capable of. But climb this vertical bank? No, I would not have asked that.

What happened next made my heart sink. Mesc lunged up the dirt bank as directed, but as she pushed off, her hind legs sank into the soft silt and remained fully extended while her front hooves and cannons landed with a thud on the top of the high bank. Her knees were flexed at 90 degree angles; the rest of her body was hanging straight down from her knees. She couldn't push with her hind legs or pull herself up with her front legs, although she did valiantly try about four times. Thankfully, Jerry bailed.

Slinky and I rushed to the scene and I slipped off. Without speaking, Jerry and I both got under Mescalero's hindquarters in the muck and tried to boost her up the bank. But 1,100 pounds of horse was just too much for us.

I wasn't in a panic, but I was in gear. I quickly stripped the saddle and blanket off Mesc; they had slid down to her loin/flank area. I heard Jerry laugh nervously. I guess there really are a million ways to handle stress.

I realized that Mesc was so bizarrely stuck that she couldn't even fall over to get free and there was nothing Jerry and I could do to help her. One of us would have to go for help. I hated to leave Mesc, but I couldn't risk sending Jerry off on Slinky. I suddenly remembered that I'd dropped Slinky's reins when I ran to Mescalero's aid. I turned to look for him and there he was, standing about 20 feet downstream, watching us curiously.

Slinky and I made a beeline for the farmhouse. Did you ever notice in a situation like this that you don't have time to think, "Will Slinky leave his buddy, Mesc? Will I be able to handle this green colt away from another horse? What if I fall off and get hurt or I have to walk and it takes me a long time to get to help?" You don't think. You just go. Hell bent for leather - except there was no leather, because I was riding bareback.

I blasted into the farmyard where my boyfriend, Richard (now my husband of 26 years) listened to my breathless tale. He told me he would get help and that I had better get back to Mescalero. "Okay, Slinky, hang in there little guy" I thought. After one more mad crash and dash through the woods, we found things pretty much as we had left them. Jerry was sitting on a rock at the river's edge and Mesc was still in a standing position with her front legs hooked over the edge of the bank.

Actually, one thing *had* changed. Mesc had figured out how to stretch her neck up and turn her muzzle sideways so she could take tiny bites of grass between her front hooves! I remember thinking, "How odd at a time like this that she would think of eating." Horses.

The minutes crawled by. After an uncomfortably long time in limbo, I finally heard a sound other than my own beating heart. It was a tractor! Two of our neighbors, J.D. and Cecil, had come with Richard, who had brought along two sturdy halters and a logging chain. We put both halters on Mescalero, attached the chain to the halters and to the bucket of the tractor. With four of us underneath her hindquarters, ready to give her a boost, Cecil lifted the bucket slightly and eased the tractor back until there was just enough tension on the chain for Mesc to brace against. Then on "Go!", Richard, Jerry, J.D. and I gave one orchestrated push. Mescalero pitched in, too, but without luck.

Cecil moved the tractor forward and we horse-lifters backed away. Everyone took a break and let the "feel" of the practice run soak in. On the second try, all six of us knew what we had to do, and we did it.

By the time I clambered up the bank, Cecil was already off the tractor and holding Mesc by her chain lead rope while she grazed nonchalantly - as if nothing out of the ordinary had just happened. She nickered wearily as I approached and turned to nuzzle me. I could tell by her eyes that she was exhausted. To my relief, except for the fact that she was covered in sweat and mud, she did not appear to be hurt.

At that point, I didn't want anyone to ride Mesc back to the farm, so Jerry and my newly "broken in" saddle caught a ride back with the tractor crew. Richard, who has always been there for me, led Slinky back while I led Mesc. The walk through the timber gave me time to wind down and let the adrenaline flush out of my system and allowed Mesc to stretch her limbs.

I really felt badly about what had happened to Mesc. I wanted to apologize somehow and make it up to her and reassure her that this would never happen again. But she made it clear to me from the moment I started leading her home that forgiveness was unnecessary. It was as if she was saying to me, "OK, what's next?" There was no anger. No distrust. No grudge. And even after that potentially damaging incident, she never refused to do anything I asked of her.

I marvel to this day at Mescalero's resiliency and matter-of-factness, and at Slinky's honesty and generosity. They and other horses since have really shown me the meaning of unconditional trust. Mutual trust is one of the most special treasures you can discover in your life with horses.

So you can borrow my pickup or even my well-worn copy of Smoky by Will James, but don't be surprised if I turn you down when you ask to ride my good horse.

Cherry Hill

Biography - Cherry is the author of 23 books on horse training and care, including Horsekeeping on a Small Acreage, 101 Arena Exercises, and The Formative Years. She has owned and trained horses since 1967, was an instructor of university equine courses for 10 years and a horse show judge for over 25 years. Cherry and her husband Richard Klimesh live in Colorado with their seven horses. Together, they are producing a video collection on horsekeeping and training. Cherry Hill's website at http://www.horsekeeping.com/ provides many articles and tips about training, riding and horse care.

A Love So Strong
Chapter Four

I Was There For The Seasons Of Life

I was there from the very beginning when he came into this world…
a little bay, struggling to get his feet underneath him in a wet chilly
world. Although it was July in Washington State, it was wet from
the ever-present rains in which his mother decided to propel him
into the world. She wouldn't head for the barn, so little Gabriel was
born out in the field. His only marking - an upward arrow-shaped
snip on the tip of his nose - spoke volumes of his desire to be in the
air, even on that first day. From the very beginning, he developed a
strong determination to get up and move, finding life a joy as he
sprang around his mamma and took his first taste of milk. And
once refreshed, he frolicked about, testing his limbs, springing into
the air before settling down to rest.

I was there for his day of separation from his mother. She took one
last look and bade him farewell as she entered the trailer to go to
her new home. He had become used to being separated from his
mom when he and I would explore the world as he was growing.
This day seemed like no big deal as she rolled down the road and
we once again went for our walk around the stables.

We were bonded together, but our bond was tested many times. For
instance, his first bath with the hose… he wanted to get away from
that hose as fast as he could, and that meant leaping into the air.
With my arms around his neck to keep us together, my legs lifted
from the ground I knew this little weanling was bound for higher

elevations. He soon settled down and the bath was over and never given a second thought.

I was there the day he took flight and sailed over his first obstacle. There just happened to be a drainage ditch separating us when I came to visit one sunny day and he wanted his treat that he knew would be in my pocket. So, over he sailed without hesitation. Realizing that jumping was fun, he tested his abilities another day, jumping the hay cart that was in the middle of the aisle as we were heading out to play in the field. Remember that little arrow on the tip of his nose… pointing straight up!

I was there the day we first put the saddle on his back. Then came the task of carrying a rider, and without a fuss he accepted that, as we had built upon our bond of trust. And although he had been telling me for the past three years that he had a fond affection for jumping, I thought it might be best to stay more rooted to the earth for a while. But as we explored more of the world in the saddle, he took every opportunity to leap logs and rocks and even the edge of the dressage arena just for fun. This was very embarrassing at his first dressage competition, but the cute little white fence looked so inviting.

I was also there when frightening things happened. Loading into a straight bumper hitch trailer for the first time one evening at the conclusion of a clinic, it started to rain and thunder. Gabriel had traveled well in many slant trailers without any problems and willingly went right in this time. It was getting darker by the minute and our friend's horse would not load. Pressure was being put on the other horse and he put up a big fuss. Gabriel began to get really nervous with the stress increasing around him. When he could take it no longer, he did the only thing he knew to do and tried to jump. He clamored into the front feeder area, which was never meant to hold a horse, and there he was stuck for what seemed an eternity to me. I screamed for the others to open the doors and I reached inside to attempt to help my frightened boy. He flung himself up to the top of the trailer again and emerged out into the night and rain with a huge gash between his front legs up under the girth area, blood pouring out. But he trusted me and we went inside to await the veterinarian for help. My poor boy had assumed that jumping was the answer to get out of a bad situation, but this time it had caused only further pain. However, our love kept us bonded and he followed me into any trailer I directed him into, despite that night.

I was there the time that he wanted to see the world from the other side of the hitching rail. Gabriel was tied to the usual hitching rail outside the tack room, which was about chest high. It was designed to be accessed from both sides and multiple horses could be tied from either side. There was always something to watch, with horses and wildlife around. As I was coming out of the tack room with my saddle in hand, I watched in horror as Gabriel gathered himself up and sprang over the rail, still tied. I just about dropped the saddle and gasped in surprise. I turned to see what it was he wanted to look at so desperately. It was another horse and rider, who were also stunned by what they had just witnessed. My little boy was a coiled spring which could leap anything at any time just to get a different perspective of life.

I was there the day we set up poles and logs which allowed him the opportunity to sail over "proper" obstacles. I felt his excitement with every approaching jump, his willingness to bound over, not even hesitating with each new challenge.

And so it went as he matured - Gabriel quietly suggesting that he would prefer to be jumping and I, feeling the desire not to take the chances which I had taken in my youth. Because I had known the thrill of jumpers, I knew what he could do. When turned out in the arena without a rider, he would happily jump the fences that were set up, as if they were there just for his pleasure. I knew it was coming; the day to let his wings spread. For Gabriel was an angel clothed in an equine body, bound for glory.

So I was there the day I let him go. We loaded him into the trailer, bound for his new life in Colorado as the jumper that he always wanted to be. Just as children grow up and we have to let them head out into the world for a life that they have prepared for, it was time to let Gabriel go. I had interviewed and turned down prospective buyers, because I was not just looking to sell a horse; rather, I was trying to find him a partner to continue his education.

Letting go was the hardest thing to do and many a tear has flowed, but I know that this is where my Gabriel is happiest.

I will be there when his career is at its peak. I like to hear the tales of the exciting adventures he is experiencing in his new life. And I will be there in the end, for sadly we all know that we are earth-bound creatures, both human and equine. But I know that some-day, my Gabriel and I will be sailing over the clouds with his head held high and his snip pointing to the glory of heaven.

Maia Bottemiller

Biography - Maia Bottemiller grew up riding horses at her grandfather's farm in Alabama. Her room as a child was filled with horse books, posters and many model horses. As a teen, she found a hunter/jumper barn nearby that exchanged riding lessons for grooming and Maia was in heaven. As she developed her love and abilities, she had the opportunity to ride many horses for private individuals. While at Washington State University, she was captain of the Equestrian Team and rode sidesaddle, rodeo drill team, saddle seat and eventing. Marrying an Air Force man, she had the opportunity to ride horses in different countries. Maia is pursuing dressage and bringing up her daughter, who continues the craze for horses.

Memoirs Of A Perfect Partnership

If we are very lucky in our lives, we will each know a horse that will change us forever. The horse in my story, Boo, was a 7/8 Thoroughbred field hunter. He was over 17-hands-high, with an incomparable mind, unforgettable disposition, stunning head, and legs and back that paid the price for his beauty and willingness. He had more mileage when I got him at 14 than most horses get in a lifetime.

"Boofus" packed me around my first novice event, over my first 3'6" course and eventually retired to my home. When I went to college, Boo became a therapy horse at the farm where I taught. He carried very ill and fragile children and adults safely. He was a phenomenal animal. So special was he, that many years and countless fine horses later, Boo frequently returns to my thoughts, where he looms as large as he ever did in life.

It occurred to me while out jogging the other day - a voice in my head posed the question that I had left unasked in the crowded blur that is my young, adult professional life: "If you could change just one thing, turn back the clock to alter just one event, what would it be?" The answer poured into my consciousness from the well where it had lain for some eight years: I would have Boo back again. I found myself amazed at the firmness of my conviction, which intensified as memories of October afternoons on my big, gray gelding pursued me down the leaf-covered trail through Rock Creek Park. Dissatisfied with my legal career, disheartened by the strife that perpetually rocks my family and painfully aware, at 28, that I might not become who I always meant to be, I know that what I want the most is to have that horse back. Even for a day.

It needn't be a day of the 14-year-old Boo; the massive, still agile form over-aweing my still-developing 14-year-old body and sensibilities. It needn't be the Boo who could fly me over a cross-country course, hands in mane, knowing that it was the power beneath me, and not within me, that made it all possible. The great galloping white presence that slowed cars on the hill in front of our pasture, just to see the fairy-tale horse come alive, a carousel giant in the flesh.

Surely as I want him back, it isn't so that he can bathe me in glory, or pride, or even the breathless fear-passion of my youth's controlled recklessness. And although in my adulthood I finally comprehend the something-more-than-unison of our quiet afternoons of flat work, his back and legs still supple, his body still submissive, yet expressive, into his late teens, I would not call him back from his rest only to ask him to give me that once more.

No, I think with my one hypothetical wish, I'd leave job and family and disrupted dreams alone for an afternoon walk with Boo, and ask only that I have him back as he was before he grew too sick to want to be alive. Before the cancer ate away the confidence in his kind eyes, before his world-wisdom was clouded by pain. I'd have him back on his terms, and spend the day stretching his legs, riding in a half-seat to preserve his back, through some fresh-cut cornfield in the November wind that fired his hunter's soul to the last day.

And the reason why is as simple as the wish: to be grateful again that this force of nature bowed to my childish aspiration to be part of it, and consented to carry me with him. And perhaps to recognize in his eyes again that I'd somehow proven worthy of the gift, so that once he evaporates back into the dream world of the past eight years, I could still gallop down the leaf-strewn path of infinite possibility that is forever beneath his feet.

Lara Schwartz

Biography - Born in New York, Lara graduated from Brown University in 1993 and from Harvard Law School in 1998. She began riding at seven-years-old, grooming Shetland Ponies and cooling off racehorses at a small Thoroughbred farm. Later, she attended a girls' school with a riding department where she learned to foxhunt, and play polo, and competed in hunter/ jumper shows and 3-day events. In college, she became a therapeutic riding instructor and also discovered dressage, which is her passion today.

"Don't cry because it's over. Smile because it happened."

Theodor Seuss Geisel

Blackie

Fifteen years ago, we were looking for a house in the country with enough acreage to keep a couple of horses. My daughter and I had taken up riding hunt seat. We were given a horse and after boarding for a year, we decided we wanted to have our own place.

We had four places picked out that were close to what we wanted and we were about to make a decision on one, when I read in the classified ads about the five-acre ranch with a barn. We went and took a look and right from the first moment I knew it was just what I had been looking for. In the pasture were a couple of horses, so I knew it was going to be fine for mine. While looking at the house, I mentioned that we only had one horse and were looking for one more to keep him company. The owner said, "If you buy the house, I will leave the black horse in the pasture for you as well." That turned out to be the best part of the deal.

Blackie, at two-years-old, was not yet broken, but would be rideable by the time we took possession of the house. It was too good to be true. A house, land, barn and horse, all for one price. In a few years, I was to find out what a great deal it truly was.

Although Blackie was gentle and seemed like a nice horse, I had another one, Vic, that demanded more of my time if I wanted to show, so my son rode Blackie. Neither of us was making any headway, so my son took Vic over and I started riding Blackie. From the very first, we were a team. He was so careful with me and after a lot of hours trail riding and street riding, we took some jumping lessons. From the first jump, it was like he knew just what to do. If there was a line, he went down the line. He never looked at the fences, he just jumped them. It was as if we were one. I had the

77

desire and he had the talent, which gave me all the confidence in the world.

My trainer moved away just as we were starting to show, so I hunted for another trainer. After training with him for six months, he told me I needed another horse to show if I wanted to win any ribbons. I knew in my heart that Blackie and I could win; I just needed to learn how to ride him to make him look good. I knew he would jump anything and that had to be half the battle. It must have been me that was keeping us out of the ribbons.

At home, Blackie was with me whenever I was outside. I would bring him out in the yard, turn him loose and he would stay close and just munch on the grass around me while I did yard work. If I was in the pasture working, he was right by my side, protecting me from the other horses who weren't allowed to come close to me. It almost seemed that he understood everything I said. We became the best of friends.

I rode every day - rain, shine or snow, it didn't matter - sometimes for 15 minutes sometimes for 10 hours. Blackie loved to be ridden. He would always come to the fence and whinny to me if he saw me, even from a window in the house. I knew he was the horse for me and I just needed a trainer to teach me how to ride him right.

At one of the shows, I saw a trainer who was really talking to his students and working with them every minute. I rode over to watch. Within a few minutes, I found myself asking if he was taking on new students. When he said yes, I asked him what he thought of Blackie. He said we were an easy fix.

Two weeks later at the next show and with only two lessons behind us, we won our first class over fences. That was just the beginning. We went on to place third and fourth in all of our divisions that year for year-end awards. The following year, Black-N-Blue (as I now called him) went on to win his first championship in non-Thoroughbred, reserve championship in adult and equitation (18 and over).

We were always in the ribbons. It might have taken the judge a class or two at a show to learn to appreciate him, but they would all come around. He was this little Paint horse competing against these big beautiful Warmbloods and Thoroughbreds, knowing he was as good as they were.

At the shows, if a child didn't have a horse to ride, or theirs came up lame or whatever, I would let them ride Blackie. I just made sure they had gentle hands and would treat him right. He would take them around a course of cross poles just like a trooper, then come back and take me over 4 ft. fences and not blink an eye. He was serious about his showing and everyone knew it. All the kids wanted to ride him. Sometimes he would show in as many as 22 classes out of 50 in a weekend.

He just loved to be played with. When we would go into the arena to do a course, I would always scratch his neck and say, "Blackie, lets go show them how it is done," and believe me, he gave 100 per cent every time. No one wanted to ride against us; he could do the medal classes without a rider. Just give him a practice round on Friday night and by Saturday he knew the striding, speed and the course. He was wonderful. He took me over the courses and all I had to do was look pretty; he would do the rest.

There was a downside to all this. Every time I would leave town for more than a couple of days, Blackie would colic. I would have to call the vet each time I was going to be away, hook up my trailer and truck and say do whatever needs to be done for him. We ran tests of all kinds and never found out why he would colic. We kept meds on hand and could always catch him early, until the time we went to Georgia for Thanksgiving. He coliced, our vet took him to another vet for surgery and when they gave him the shot to sedate him for surgery, he passed away.

That day, I lost a part of me I will never get back. He was the truest of friends, always listened, never argued, always loved and gave of himself to the fullest. The weeks following his death I was devastated, then the letters, cards, drawings and even statues and pictures started coming in from all the kids from other farms that we had showed against. I realized he had touched more than my life; he had touched each and every one that ever saw him show.

The little freebee horse with a heart of gold was never for sale. I turned down offers of over $20,000.00 for him without blinking. My husband thought I was crazy. I knew I could never replace him, so no price would have ever been enough. He was truly a one of a kind and loved by all that had the fortune of knowing him.

I tried showing my five-year-old Trakehner/TB as a hunter-jumper, but my heart wasn't in it. I knew that in order to keep showing, I needed to change disciplines and find something we could do and have fun with. Poetry-N-Motion is big and beautiful and we did finish the season with two championships, one reserve and a third place, but I felt as though we never had a really good round like I had on Blackie. I know he has class and is a pretty mover, so we are trying dressage. My dressage instructor thinks he has international potential and has been working with him. Now we have to work on *me* and get me to the same level. We are doing much better and both enjoying our new endeavor, but have a long way to go.

I feel very privileged to have owned such a great horse as Blackie and I believe I may now have my second. When I consider that some people never find the right horse and I will have owned two, I am indeed very lucky. I will always remember the little black horse that showed a whole organization it wasn't about a price tag - it was about devotion and love.

Peggy A. Gwin

Biography - Peggy and her husband Roger live in Vicksburg Michigan with their five horses, dogs, cats and a couple of boarded horses. Their daughter Angel continues to event. Peggy hopes to retire to a warmer climate in a few years and continue to raise Trakehner/TB horses. She wants to show dressage and train the babies, then pass them along to her daughter to event with. "We hope to move close to each other and enjoy our love of horses for he rest of our lives. There will always remain a special place in my heart for my Black-N-Blue and someday we will be together again."

Diablo, My Best Friend

My horse is very special. His name is Diablo.
He is nine-years-old and used to belong to my Aunt Teresa, but
now he is my first horse.
He has a special place in my heart that is filled with love and joy.
He has become my best friend.

One day, I told him that I would give him his feed and hay only if
he put his head over the fence so that I could pet him.
At first, he turned his head away as if he did not want me to pet
him.
When he did that I just did the same.
As soon as I turned away, he started to nuzzle me on my neck to
get my attention.
I was surprised and I started to pet him and talk to him until it
was dark.

Now when I go outside to feed him,
if I am sad, lonely, depressed, or just need a good friend, he helps
by nuzzling me.
I don't think that anyone or any other horse can take the place
that Diablo has in my heart.
He makes me feel special when I am around him and when I am
riding him.
To me, he is an understanding horse that I believe in all the way.
Even if I looked all over the world, I don't think that I could find
a horse that fills me with more love and joy than my horse,
Diablo.

April Douglas, age 11

Biography - April Douglas. "I am 12-years-old and will be in the seventh grade in the fall. Away from my school activities, I enjoy rodeo events, riding and taking care of my horse (Diablo), shopping, being with my friends and family, and of course, watching TV. If you're a trail rider, you may know my Paw Paw. His name is Michael Mason and he is the owner/publisher of the Trail Rider Magazine. My mom, Kim is the executive editor. Their web site is www.trailridermagazine.com; email address is trailmag@centurytel.net or phone # is 800-448-1154. If you haven't seen this magazine, tell them I said to send you a free issue! They'll be glad to do it."

"Every problem has a gift for you in its hands."

Richard Bach

Elizabeth And Ginger

It was bone-chilling cold on that first Saturday morning of the New Year - one of those Midwest winter days when staying in a warm bed was more valuable to me than all the money in the world. Unfortunately, the phone rang early, there were horses to feed, ice to break out of water buckets and the girls were coming over at 9:00 a.m.

When I was in my early teens, my trainer had encouraged me to spend my entire Saturday at the barn. I loved every minute of it and vowed that when I had a barn of my own, I would offer the same opportunity to my students. Today, the five regulars arrived right on time, as always. Cheven, Elizabeth, Beth, Denise and Sherry were all wearing English riding boots just visible underneath their heavy winter trousers. All were buried in hats, coats, scarves and gloves so thick that it was hard to tell who was who.

Connie had gotten me out of bed that morning to ask if she could bring over an older mare that had been forgotten by her owner and left to fend for herself in a barren field. Even though I certainly didn't need another mouth to feed, my good friend knew that I couldn't say no. I knew what it felt like to be given a leg up just when you were sure it was all over and to pay back my debt, I took in strays - stray dogs, horses, ponies and people. That day, I would meet a stray that would change all of our lives forever.

After a morning of riding, mucking stalls and cleaning tack, the girls and I settled in to have lunch. Soon after, still enjoying the warmth of my barn office, sipping down the last of our hot choco-late, we heard a truck pull into the driveway. I had told everyone that there was a new horse coming in and I was going to try to find a good home for her. The girls scrambled to put their hats and gloves on and were out the door like a shot.

It had been unusually cold that winter and the driveway was like a skating rink, making it hard to get the 150 feet to and from the house each day to feed and teach. There in the driveway sat an old, dented red pickup that had seen better days. Standing in the bed of the truck was the skinniest horse I had ever seen. Her coat was long and dull and in spite of the length of her hair, there was no mistaking the fact that you could count all the major bones in her body. Connie stepped out of the passenger's side of the old pickup and the horse owner stepped out of the driver's side. I welcomed them both and even though I wanted to horse whip this man, after seeing the condition he had allowed the mare to get into, I instead thanked him for taking the time to do right by her.

Without a word, he dropped the tailgate, grabbed the lead line that was hanging from her ill-fitting halter and asked her to jump down onto the icy driveway. She was too weak to argue and nearly fell to her knees while exiting the bed of the truck. He handed me the lead line and headed for his truck. We briefly shook hands at the truck door and I never saw the man again.

"What a sack of bones!" Denise exclaimed. All the girls were shocked by what they saw as we came into the barn, except Elizabeth. "She may not be as fat as you are, Denise, but she is beautiful just the same." With that said, Elizabeth ran over to the new mare and threw her arms around her neck, welcoming her to the farm. "You're home. We are going to fatten you up, brush you, take good care of you and someday soon, you are going to be the most beautiful horse in the barn."

I was so moved by the instant connection the pair made that I invited Elizabeth to name the mare. It was as if they had known each other forever. Before the mare had been in the barn for five minutes, Elizabeth exclaimed, "Ginger. That is what I will call her and when she fattens up and her coat slicks out, she will be the color of ginger snaps." The other girls laughed and poked fun at Elizabeth for thinking that the bag of bones would ever look pretty, but there was no changing Elizabeth's mind. She somehow knew that Ginger would get better and transform herself into a beautiful horse. Elizabeth was prepared to make sure that it happened.

Ginger was not the first stray I had taken in over the years, but there was certainly something different about her. Even the toughest livestock men in town were interested in this old mare. When Reither stopped by the next day for his usual cup of coffee and to watch me clean stalls, I brought him over to see Ginger. He was a retired pig farmer and he knew the ins and outs of fattening up livestock prior to sending them to the slaughterhouse. "Who the hell lets a horse get like this?" Reither asked. "I don't know Reither," I replied. "All I know is that I'm glad he brought her over and didn't leave her to die in that field."

Reither stayed by Ginger's stall while I returned to cleaning the stall next door. "You know, Reither, you could grab a pitchfork and give me a hand!" I said, laughing. Reither sipped his coffee and remarked, "Look, I'm not the fool who bought a horse farm in Indiana. You just carry on; you're doing a grand job! Besides, I did my fair share of cleaning stalls over the past 80 years and my work is done. I'll just stand here and watch you." This grizzled old man started to bring Ginger carrots each morning.

Even 84-year-old Al, who had slaughtered cows, pigs and farmed for most of those years, felt sorry for the mare and started to find excuses to swing by several times a day over the coming months. I think both men knew what it was like to be used up and thrown away. In an odd way, Ginger represented both of their lives and at least for her, I think they both hoped the story would have a different ending.

Tom, our local vet, came out the next day to look at Ginger and assess her overall condition. He agreed that she was the skinniest horse he had ever seen and estimated her age at well over 20 years. This confirmed what I had already suspected. She was old enough to be someone's grandmother and was left to starve in a cold field. It shouldn't be like this, ever. Tom cautioned me to feed her small amounts of food until her digestive tract was acclimated. He also warned me that she was weakened by the experience and may never be rideable. I heard him well enough, but thought to myself, "Ginger old girl, you and I are going to prove Tom wrong. I don't care what I have to do; by God, you are going to make it."

Over the next few months, an almost miraculous transformation occurred, not only in Ginger, but also in everyone who spent time with her - and there were plenty of people who spent time with her. Her stall started to resemble a tourist attraction with students, neighbors, retired farmers and friends stopping by every day to groom her, feed her carrots and apples, or just visit with her.

However, no one spent more time with Ginger than Elizabeth. She actually convinced her school bus driver to change the bus route so she could come over immediately after school every night. She would quickly change into her barn clothes; pick up an armload of brushes and carrots and head into the stall with Ginger, shutting the door behind her. Many nights I would sneak into the barn to check on the pair, only to hear Elizabeth talking to Ginger as though they were having a normal conversation. This is what life is supposed to be like, I would think to myself. A quiet barn, twenty good horses all in their stalls nibbling on the last bits of their dinner and one young girl sharing time with her favorite horse, as you would spend time with a best friend.

As winter faded into spring, Ginger had blossomed into a swell-looking little mare, just as Elizabeth had vowed she would. In the time that Ginger spent with us, she and Elizabeth taught us all about unconditional love, and about looking beyond outward appearances to see the real beauty within. Their devotion to each other had rallied an entire community. We all rooted for them in our own ways and for our own reasons.

Soon Ginger would be healthy enough to go to a new home. I called Elizabeth's mother and asked if they would consider taking Ginger, because the pair had become such good friends. After some deliberation at their end, her parents agreed and we started to make plans for Ginger to become Elizabeth's first horse. To read more about Elizabeth and Ginger, see Horse Tales for the Soul Volume Two...

Bonnie Marlewski-Probert

Biography - Bonnie Marlewski-Probert is a professionally trained horseman with 20 years of safe, responsible teaching and training experience. She has published more than 1000 magazine articles, several books and videos for horse lovers around the world. To learn more about Bonnie's work, visit her web site at TheCompletePet.com. To order books, call 800-700-5096 or order via the web site.

Itsy Bitsy

About three years ago, a horse named Itsy Bitsy came to the farm where I was riding. He was a Quarter Horse that had been used for Western riding, but he ended up on an English riding farm. I am lucky that he did, or I would never have learned the love you find for a horse.

Itsy must have been abused at his old home, for when he got to the farm, he was very skittish and head-shy. He would never have the class to make a fancy show horse, but he had the personality to make a great friend. That is exactly what we became. I helped work with him and before long, a bond formed between us. He eventually let me stroke his face and touch him when other people would startle him. I was eventually the only one who could ride him.

After working with him for a few good months, everyone started to see a major improvement. Even though Itsy was still very cautious about his head, he would allow people to touch him. I still had to help put his bridle on, because I was the only one that could get close enough to his face to do it. People started riding him and falling in love with him. All the little beginners always wanted to ride him. Eventually, he became a school horse. I still rode him every so often, but I had other horses to ride and Itsy was very busy too.

After a year, Itsy was being used for lessons all the time. I started to show him in lower level dressage and we placed very well. Although he could not go much higher because of the brands on his hindquarters, he amazed many people. Whenever people saw me on Itsy, they would just laugh and say stuff about him being a plow mule.

One day, when I was riding another horse, I overheard people talking about Itsy Bitsy being for sale. I was frantic. Never in my life did I think I could be separated from him. Eventually that day came and has long since gone. Itsy is now being ridden in dressage shows and is used as a pleasure horse. He is very well taken care of and gets a lot of love and attention. Although I do not see him very often, I still get to ride him from time to time. I taught him a lot and in exchange he taught me how to love a horse, even if he may not be your "dream horse."

The day he came into my life was a dream come true. It seemed as if he was an angel and just needed someone to love him. I hope he keeps his same personality and gives other people some hope in their life, too.

Megan K. Gravett

Biography - Megan K. Gravett. "I have been riding for eight years. I primarily do dressage, but will occasionally do some jumping. I love horses and I hope to be an equine veterinarian some day. I do not own a horse, but I ride many. Besides being at the farm as much as I can, I enjoy swimming on a swim team and hanging out with my friends."

Brumby

I've read many stories about first horses:
"My first horse was so perfect, she would do anything for me."
"My pony was perfectly trained and did everything perfectly."
Well, my first, a 13-hand Palomino Welsh-type pony, was trained in the school of Marx. Not Karl, but Harpo, Chico and Groucho Marx. He took his teaching style from Groucho, but his personality was more that of Harpo.

I was a very novice 14-year-old, raised on books by Sewell, Farley and Will James. The message in all those books tended to be, "If you love your horse enough, it will do anything for you!" Brumby loved that attitude!

He'd gone through a short string of innocent little girls by the time I got him as a nine-year-old. He earned his new name, "Brumby", the Australian wild horse, by seeing to it that I fell off whenever I made a mistake, which was every day for the first month. Mind you, he never *threw* me off. He merely took me to the level of my incompetence and let nature take its course. Nature usually landed me on my tush.

Brumby had a series of steps he took any rider through to test the level of the rider's ability. It took me about a month just to master level one, which was a killer trot combined with a quick halt.

The killer trot consisted of refusing to break into a canter and simply trotting faster and faster until it became so rough that the rider lost all control and slid slowly sideways off Brumby's round shoulder. The quick halt is, I'm sure, familiar to most riders. I'd get him into a canter, and then he'd stop dead, head slightly lowered, so I wasn't thrown over his head, but against his neck, to again experience the slow slide to the ground.

Of course, it didn't help that the western saddle that came with Brumby was moldy and nailed together. Within a short time, I stopped using a saddle and rode bareback instead.

After that first month of sliding off daily (or more often), getting dragged because I was too stubborn to let go of the reins, taking tumbles, getting my head bonked (without a helmet. This was in the dark ages when kids were still expendable and the helmet I'd been given as a nine-year-old had become tight enough to have been used as an instrument of torture during the Spanish Inquisition.) I decided that if my parents realized how often I was falling off, they might insist that I get rid of the horse. It didn't occur to me that they might insist on more riding lessons. There were no instructors in the area, anyway, since the local stable where I'd ridden at age seven had closed after the owner broke his back.

I decided I'd better figure out a way to stay safe.

My favorite horse authors had me convinced that if I got "mean" with my horse, I'd lose his love forever. But I finally decided I didn't have his love to begin with. I was his favorite diversion. He loved going for rides. If I went out to the pasture without his bridle (just treats such as grain), he'd turn his back on me, make motions that I interpreted as threats to kick and wouldn't let me touch him. So I took him for a ride almost daily, and for the sake of my health I needed to do something fast!

Prevailing attitudes at the time were simply "show them who's boss." I felt that was wrong, and there must be better ways. But at the time, there were no modern trainers in the area, and I found no training articles other than the cowboy versions suggesting use of force.

On the next ride, when he pulled a quick stop that sent me flying in front of him, I got up and lit into him. I bellowed, yanked him several times, slapped him across the chest with the reins…I felt so mean. Later, he dragged me. I'd done the usual gentle roll off the shoulder, but hung onto the reins when he took off for the barn. I bounced along behind, bellowing, then resorted to lots of yelling and wholloping him with the reins when I finally regained my feet.

I figured that was it. Now he'd *never* love me.

But that day, when I took off the bridle, instead of kicking up his heels and tearing off into the pasture, he hung around. He rubbed his head on me, followed me around and nuzzled me gently. The next day when he saw me, he actually whinnied a greeting!

Brumby lesson number one: he can't love me until he can respect me. And he can't respect me until he can trust me to keep us both safe. He was teaching me to listen. Even if I'd made a mistake, at least I was listening. From this point on, Brumby started being gentler in his lessons.

It actually took more than a year to learn that important lesson, but it was an important life lesson. The old expression "show them who's boss" never went over well with me, and Brumby showed me it wasn't "show them who's boss", it was "prove to them that you *will* keep both of you safe." When I started listening to Brumby and mastering his lessons, he began to respect me.

There were many girls in my rural area who "loved" horses, but I didn't understand them. They would gush about how much they loved their horse, then a year or two later, they would be buying a new horse, explaining, "I outgrew my horse" or "She wasn't winning enough ribbons" or "I needed a better horse."

I honestly didn't know how to answer the question, "why don't you get rid of Brumby and get a better horse?" He's *my horse*. He's like my brother, my uncle, my cousin, or my dad. How do you "get rid" of a family member?

A year after I got Brumby, I bought a yearling Appaloosa/Morgan/ light draft mix filly. Mom wanted me to have two horses so she or others could ride with me. This new filly, Shawnie, was perfect for a youngster who still knew nothing and wasn't aware that she knew nothing. Shawnie had never been handled much when I got her, but I led her the seven miles home. My idea of groundwork was leading her along on just about every ride I took with Brumby. I also took Shawnie on walks on a lead rope around my country area. We'd walk for miles while she got used to cars and tractors, barking dogs and kids on bikes. I trained her to ride without benefit of a professional trainer, except Brumby. He was excellent. Brumby was on his best behavior when we had Shawnie with us. Both Shawnie and I were so innocent that we had no idea that anything could go wrong - therefore, nothing did!

Brumby followed me to college along with our four-year-old filly. We moved from rural upstate New York to the big city of Tucson, Arizona. Mom and I trailered the horses cross-country ourselves. Each evening when we rode them, Brumby would turn east and break into a brisk trot.

I moved them into a stable near desert trails on the Rollito River. Brumby was the type of strong equine character who picked up nicknames wherever he went: Bramble face, the General, Little Man, and from the stable owner, That Pony (who should be dog meat!). I don't think he liked outgoing equines smarter than himself. I had warned the owner when we arrived at the stable that Brumby was an escape artist. He stated firmly that *no* horses escaped his pens! It took a full month, but Brumby did prove him wrong. The owner's wife, Joy, admitted to me one morning that she and her husband had been summoned to the barn by their stallion's screaming and banging, only to find Brumby loose and standing on top of hay bales in the open shed, the morning sun streaming onto his golden coat! Brumby proceeded to lead them on a merry chase until his regular feeding time arrived, at which time he allowed them to catch him and take him back to his paddock. Joy found it quit amusing. Her husband did not.

At first I was insecure with my limited knowledge of riding and my mutt horses. Most of the others at the stable were competent riders with well-trained show horses. But I met others on my desert treks and began riding with them. Shawn and I muddled through, but Brumby shone with his own light. We met two girls with western pleasure Quarter Horses who were amazed that Brumby could lift his feet over the 18 inch high barrier that kept motorbikes out of one of the desert trails. We rode with the Thoroughbred who was afraid to go downhill, the Quarter Horse who was afraid of saguaro cactuses, and the tender-footed Appaloosa who couldn't walk in rocky areas even with shoes. Nothing phased Brumby. Whatever came his way, he dealt with it and even made it fun.

Brumby spent the rest of his life in upstate New York. He continued to escape, played gentle tricks on the vets and farrier, and befriended an adopted Death Valley burro I had taken in. Most people have someone they can identify as a mentor in their life. There are plenty of important people in my life, but a feisty, 13-hand Palomino pony was my mentor. He demanded that I listen to him, and instead of "getting rid of him," or "teaching him who's boss," I chose to listen. Brumby taught me about horses, he taught me about trust and he taught me about life. He showed me with his Harpo Marx humor that "Life is what you make of it. Make it fun!"

To read more Brumby stories, check out Horse Tales for the Soul, Volume Two.

Barbara J. Linsley

Biography - Barbara J. Linsley. "I have loved horses from the time I could distinguish what they were. Brumby came to me when I was 14 years-old, followed a year later by a yearling, Shawnda. Shawnie is now 30 and shares her pasture with my other elder mare and our adopted donkey. I have found the two horses who will see me through the second half of my life, a three-year-old Morgan, brimming with fun and personality, and my newest, a gentle little Appaloosa weanling. I share what my horses have taught me with my fifth grade students at Mt. Markham School in West Winfield, NY. Barbara can be reached at PO Box 5, N. Brookfield, NY 13418.

Gratitude

Chapter Five

Amigo Mio

Amigo was the result of a mismatched romance between an American Saddlebred sire and a little gray Mustang mare.

Anxious to rid themselves of the illegitimacy, the not-so-proud owners offered the two- month-old foal to my father in return for hauling him away. My mother took pity on the gangly little foal, and fearing a bleak future for him, they converted the trunk of their '39 Pontiac and hauled him home to be raised on the same formula as his human counterpart, my older brother. They named him Amigo Mio.

A racehorse trainer by trade, my father was serving his civil duty during WWII at a shipyard in Napa, California. Until Amigo was a four-year-old, he had my dad's undivided attention in his formative training.

At the close of the war, anxious to return to the track, father resigned from his position at shipyard. Amigo was ready to embark on what would become a 15-year career as my Dad's personal pony horse.

By 1945, the little "accident" had matured into a 16-hand, blue roan gelding weighing in excess of 1,200 pounds. His size and bulk, as well as his attitude, played a big part in his ability to perform his duties as a faithful and dependable side-kick in breaking two-year-olds for their racing careers.

Used exclusively as a companion to the two-year-olds in training, Amigo gained a reputation with the exercise boys as being the only pony horse they would trust alongside the green and often exuberant Thoroughbreds.

Among Amigos' many attributes, speed was not one of them. If father had to pick up a runaway colt down the home stretch, he would position Amigo accordingly and time the approach of the colt to get a head start. During this burst, which lasted for about 150 yards, Dad would reach down and grab the runaway. Amigo's sheer bulk and natural loss of forward momentum would slow them both down.

During one of the race meets, my dad had an accident resulting in a broken thumb, and was encased by a cast that ran clear up his right arm. Unable to hold the horse he was ponying, (which is exercising another horse by leading him at a walk, trot, or gallop), my father taught Amigo to pony with no reins, enabling the free use of his left hand to hold the horse he was ponying on the right with his left hand. Amigo got so good at this that in his free time my dad would show him off by loping down the home stretch, switching leads every few strides with no bridle whatsoever.

Amigo was joined so well at my father's hip, that my dad only had to think about what he wanted from his sidekick and it was done. A favorite pastime in the early mornings, while Amigo waited patiently for his charge to come off the track to be escorted back to the barn, would be to wrap the reins around the saddle horn and then ask Amigo who he wanted to say good morning to. With hidden cues from Lawrence, Amigo would side pass to and approach one of any given number of fellow race trackers/trainers. The chosen individual would brag to those less fortunate that he alone was Amigo's favorite. One of the trainers who was "chosen" more often than the others offered my dad $1,500 for the big gelding. That was a lot of money in those days. My mother put her foot down and forbade my father to sell her horse.

Not without vices, Amigo enjoyed a cold bottle of beer in the afternoons with his partner after a hard day's work.

Nor was Amigo to be confused with "Mr. Milquetoast". At one of the race meets, a new trainer stalled his stud next to Amigo. The gentleman approached and advised that if my dad thought anything at all of his pony horse, now would be the time to move him to another stall. My dad surveyed the situation and noted that the stall walls didn't go clear to the ceiling of the barn, in fact, they were low enough that the horses on either side, could reach over the top if so inclined. Being a good neighbor, in return he advised the naive trainer that if he thought anything of his stud, now would be the time to move him. The stranger shrugged, said something about giving fair warning and walked off. The next morning the stallion and stranger were gone.

By the time I was old enough to remember Amigo, who was eight years my senior, he was already so much a part of the family that in retrospect, I realize I regarded him as more of an older brother than anything else. He was the first horse I ever had contact with, and he raised me well. If I disappeared from view, mama could almost be sure to find me in Amigo's stall.

My biggest thrill was to ride behind my dad in the early mornings on Amigo to the track to watch the horses exercise. When father had to go to the racing secretary's office, he'd say, "Your guys wait here, I'll be right back."

Upon his return, Amigo and I hadn't moved from where he left us. So proud of myself for taking care of Amigo in my father's absence, the enormity of the situation didn't dawn on me until years later. In addition his regular duties, Amigo was a qualified babysitter.

By the time they retired from the track in 1960, the illegitimate little foal, who had less than a bright future, had acquired a reputation as everyone's friend. While he was never going to be a racehorse, he became as big a legend in his own right as any Kentucky Derby winner.

Lynne Swank-Wilder

Biography – Lynne Swank-Wilder lives in Northern California with her two Arabians and husband, Bill Wilder. Dedicated to rehabbing mishandled horses together with realizing the importance of educating the horse owner, she has given hundreds of lessons addressing the "how to" of horse training. Through her video, "Overcoming the Obstacles," Lynne has found a catalyst to share the rudiments of opening a line of communication between rider and horse. As a published writer, her articles address the process of training in layman's terms. Semi-retired, Lynne enjoys riding her own horses and working with a select group of students. To order her video, visit http://trak.to/horseclubconnection or call, Roundpen Supply, The Trail Less Traveled at (800) 317-3682. You can reach Lynne at lswank@compuserve.com.

Learning From Horses: Mama

Everything I've learned about communicating with horses, I've learned from horses. Sometimes it took awhile for the lessons they were teaching me to sink in. But the wisdom they shared with me gradually accumulated and became the system we now teach at Meredith Manor. Particular horses stand out in my memory.

One was an old-style, liver chestnut Quarter Horse mare, with those bulgy muscles and little feet, who was already doing a lot of things before we bought her to show. She had high withers, the kind that are good for holding a saddle when you're roping or cutting. She had a rather plain, coarse head that might have been ugly, except that she had a really soft eye that made you forgive the rest. Her registered name was WMD Aloha and the guy we bought her from called her Mother. That got shortened to "Mama" and Mama she was for the rest of her life.

Mama never got overly excited. I remember one time, I was pulling a homemade trailer behind a six-cylinder Chevy truck. In those days, most of the trailers were homemade and nobody thought of putting springs under them. They were pretty much wooden boxes bolted to axles and the ride must have been pretty rough. The trailer came unhitched when the truck bottomed out going over the crest of a hill and it started to pass me. I managed to block it with the truck and get it stopped so I could rehitch. There wasn't a sound from the trailer. Mama was as calm as anything, although the sweat was pouring off her. When Mama got worried, she'd sweat - but that was all.

This incident was even more remarkable when I learned from her previous owner that she had been in a trailer once that had been hit by a truck. Mama spent an hour in the overturned trailer until they got her out. I always marveled that she'd get back in a trailer at all after all that, but Mama was always compliant.

Mama was a great arena horse. Whatever the game was, she knew the drill and she'd just go along. It didn't matter if the rider was flopping around; that was okay. It didn't matter if you gave her the wrong cues; she'd ignore them and do her job. I came to really admire Mama because, pretty or not, she was so honest about doing her job, no matter what that might be. We rented her out for classes, because all anybody had to do was sit in the saddle and hold the reins. They'd be fine and might even get a ribbon.

My point about Mama is that sometimes a horse can be so honest, uncomplicated and unshakable by whatever you throw at them that you begin to think *you're* pretty good. Horses like Mama make you think you're someplace even when you haven't gone anywhere yet.

Then along comes the next horse and you find you haven't really got the vocabulary to talk to them and explain what you want them to do. People who buy a really trained horse with the notion that the horse is going to teach them what they need to know are missing the point. The horse can teach them what the right thing *feels* like, but the horse can't teach them how to communicate that same feel to another horse. That's a different skill.

Horse shows are just games people play to have fun with their horses. And as soon as somebody gets really good at the game and starts winning all the ribbons, somebody else decides to change the game so that other people have a chance to win.

A true horseman understands how to create a corridor of pressures that create a shape the horse can feel. Those corridors are the same, no matter what game the horse is being trained to play, whether he's a baby or an old campaigner or whether he's an Arab or a Quarter Horse.

You can be a true horseman without necessarily being a winner in the show game. But the people who win all the performance games are not necessarily true horsemen. They may just be riding Mama.

Ron Meredith
President, Meredith Manor International Equestrian Centre

Biography - Ron Meredith began his professional horse career in 1957 training Arabians and was a noted competitor, judge and clinician for many years in several disciplines. Ron refers to himself as a born-again horseman. "Over the years, I began to question many of the training practices I learned in the 1950s and 1960s," he says, referring to those techniques now known as "hostage training." Ron refined his ideas into a "horse logical" system of training that turns horses into willing, trusting partners. In 1963, he founded Meredith Manor International Equestrian Centre (www.meredithmanor.com; 800-679-2603) as a place where he could teach others to be competent trainers and riding instructors. Ron's contributions as an equestrian educator were recognized by Salem-Teikyo University in 1981, when he received an Honorary Doctorate of Equestrian Studies degree.

A Person Who Influenced Me

As I walk into the barn each morning and look at my horses, I wonder where they would be if I had not brought them home with me. Warrior was bought from the Western New York Equine Sanctuary as a weanling. Would he still be alive if I had not bought him? Would he have gotten a different home? Freddy was given to me by a guy that I know. Where would he be if I had not brought him home?

I was inspired to bring all these horses home by a lady I know well. Carol Ann Piazza, the owner of the Western New York Equine Sanctuary, has been a great inspiration to me since I met her three years ago. She spends her days caring for the horses that someone else didn't want any more. Every day she gets up and does what I do, I guess. The difference is that she has more horses to take care of, and some of them have difficult problems to deal with. Also, there are different horses in the barn with each passing day, week and month. Another thing Carol does is to try and rescue horses, and then find safe, caring homes for them.

Some of these horses are retired racehorses. Others are horses that were sent to auctions to be sold to the highest bidder. Often, their buyer would be someone who would buy them just to sell them for meat. Carol goes to the auctions expressly to rescue horses from a gloomy future - if there is a for them future at all. For some of the auction horses, there will be a short trip to the slaughter houses, or they will shift between owners for a while. There are also horses that have been abused or neglected.

Carol also saves foals that are by-products of the pharmaceutical industry. They are born from mares that are bred for the sole purpose of collecting their urine to make the drug called Premarin, a hormone substitute for women going though menopause. The foals are a dispensable part of this process and are disposed of. At three to five months of age, they are shipped to auctions, where they are primarily bought for slaughter for human consumption or sold to dog and cat food manufactures. Of course a lucky few go to homes.

Most only achieve this with help from rescuers like Carol and others, who try to rescue as many as possible. After they are brought to the sanctuary, they are returned to good health and placed in a good home where they will be cared for.

Carol is an inspiration to all horse lovers. Not many people would spend most of their lives saving the lives of the horses that have a dim future. Not many people would give all they have to living creatures that have felt no love for so long, and just need a little love and hope for the future. She is an inspiration to me, and I hope to someday to be like her and save the lives of these great animals.

Jonalee Kagels

Biography - Jonalee Kagels. " I am 16-years-old, and I have lived in New York all my life. I have two brothers, and I live on a farm with my Mom and enjoy every day of it. I have loved horses as long as I can remember. I have had my two horses, Warrior and Freddy, for about two-and-a-half years. I compete in local horse shows in western and gymkhana classes. Besides horses, I have lambs, rabbits, dogs, cats, and guinea pigs. I hope to become a veterinarian or a horse trainer - or both - and some day I would like to compete in professional barrel racing events

They Earned A Good Retirement!

As I sit on my front porch with newspaper and coffee cup in hand, I am looking out at our small front pasture at the four horses grazing there. How did we end up with so many horses to feed as we approach our "retirement" years? We have two grown sons off working on their own, a daughter in her second year at the Air Force Academy and another 13-year-old son still at home.

Our horses Rosie, Rocky, Modoc and Kiowa range in age from 18 to 22. Rocky, the oldest, has been in our family since he was six months old. He belonged first to my dad and then my brother before working his way to our son, Justin. He now belongs to our 13-year-old son, Danny.

I can still remember the Christmas day I presented Rosie to my daughter, Crystal. What a "presentation" it was! The whole family got up early to open presents. My husband, Tom, sneaked out to the barn to bring Rosie around to the front of the house for the big surprise. We stuck the biggest red bow we could find right in the middle of her forehead; I think she kind of liked being all dressed up. We called Crystal outside and I presented her with Rosie. Crystal just looked at me with tears in her eyes and said, "Really?" I could only whisper "yes" because I was so choked up at her excitement at receiving her first horse. Rosie had been my horse, but I knew she and Crystal belonged together. Most of the time, if I couldn't find Crystal I would just look for Rosie and there they would be.

Modoc belongs to my husband and Kiowa is my riding horse. During the summers, Danny and Rocky compete in local gymkhanas. I have had horses my whole life and still enjoy trail riding. While the kids were growing up, I always knew where to find them . . . out in the barn or the arena with the horses. Crystal and Justin were the real horse fans in our family. Adam, our oldest, would only ride occasionally, as he was into shooting baskets and pitching no-hitters.

If I went to town, as I would drive back down our road, there would be Crystal and Justin training one of the horses for an upcoming horse show or rodeo event. Or they might be herding the dairy cows on our neighbor's ranch or just having fun with friends on a trail ride. Many times they would invite one of their friends from town to ride one of our other horses. We liked the kids having their friends over to ride and help exercise all the horses. That way, the horses would always be settled down when us old folks wanted to saddle up for a trail ride.

So here I sit on the front porch, watching those horses that gave my children so much pleasure and taught them so much as they were growing up. My children know the value of hard work. When a lot of their friends were watching Saturday morning cartoons, mine were usually out washing a horse for a show or parade. On Friday nights, my kids were cleaning tack and ironing their clothes in preparation for the next day's event. This was not for the big breed or open shows, but for shows at a friend's boarding stable, a riding club or for 4-H. You see, we did not have fancy registered animals; just plain "backyard" horses that helped me raise my kids.

Crystal and Justin were responsible for the care and training of their own horses. They might rent a video, read a book, learn something by watching someone else or from 4-H. They even learned a few things from me! But most importantly, they spent time, lots of time - hours of riding, grooming, cleaning, and whatever else was required. They each took an ordinary horse and turned it into a dependable partner for the show ring, drill team, gymkhana events or trail riding. They won ribbons, trophies, jackets, mugs and equipment. They learned to be self-sufficient, dependable and caring people. As I look back on the paths that some of their friend's followed, I am sure those horses had a profound influence on my children, and saved me from more than a few gray hairs worrying about where my kids were and what they might be doing . . . all I had to do was look out the window toward the barn. We owe those horses a lot, not the least of which is a "retirement" where they are still loved and cared for.

I do not resent at all the fact that on most days, our four horses just stand around in the pasture, waiting to be fed and enjoying the warm sunshine. I think they've earned it! They were there to keep my children off the streets and out of trouble. But their story does not stop here; we live only 14 miles from the Air Force Academy and our daughter's classmates have discovered our horses. So most weekends, someone is here to go riding. Our horses are giving a whole new group of young people a chance to ride and learn about taking care of animals. I guess they aren't officially retired *yet*!

Roxene Ballard

Biography - Roxene Ballard. "I live on 20 acres in Black Forest, Colorado, with my husband of 33 years, and our four "semi-retired" horses. We have four children and I have been lucky to be married to a really great guy for all these years. He is now an avid horseman and even showed in western pleasure for the first time last summer. I can't remember a time when I did not love horses. I showed mostly in Northern California while growing up. It was a time when a "backyard" horse was still considered competition in the show ring. When we retire, we hope to open part of our place as a bed & breakfast with stabling facilities for travelers with horses."

A Modern Day Roundup

A roundup! We were all excited. The neighbours were moving their cattle home from pasture and we'd been invited to help out. Our young boys had just started riding horses and we had one on loan so that we could all take part. The trip would be about ten miles - some roads, some fields.

It was quite the entourage as we started out. Cows and calves, horses and riders, including one rodeo cowboy hero, four-wheelers, half ton trucks, two-way radios and me with my video camera, pulling a horse trailer for the stragglers. A modern-day roundup, complete with modern-day technology – with horses for nostalgia.

Our daughter was still an infant, so my husband, Bob, and I were to take turns riding and driving. I was to drive first. I started video taping the journey as we headed west down the road. People and cattle spread out over the road and ditches. The cattle moved along nicely and we all enjoyed visiting with our neighbours.

We hadn't gone half a mile before our first calamity. One of the neighbours was riding the ditch on his four-wheeler, talking up to the horsemen on the road, when his front wheels dropped down suddenly and he flew over the handlebars and somersaulted into the ditch. So much for modern technology over the old "horse" method! The ATV riders did more road riding and the horses moved to the ditches – and everyone paid more attention. And I missed catching any of it on film.

About halfway along, we headed south through a quarter section pasture. I took the road around so I wouldn't wake the baby with the bumps and to set myself up to continue recording the occasion on video. I was excited about filming a stampede, as the cattle moved rapidly towards me after having been turned from heading the wrong way. They soon settled down and I put the camera away and looked around for my guys. Bob had been having trouble holding his horse from the very beginning and was galloping up on the herd. I was quite a distance off, but quickly spotted my son, Ian, on his pony. Then I spied my other son, Chris, and one lone cow.

As I watched from a distance, the cow butted Chris' horse and almost unseated him. This must have made his horse angry, because she turned on the cow, charging and kicking. Fortunately, Chris hung on. Unfortunately, Ian's pony kept trying to stay close to Chris' horse. The cow was larger than his pony and he could be seriously injured if she turned on him the same way. My heart was in my mouth as I watched helplessly. Luckily, the men noticed and moved in quickly to divert the cow. Even our rodeo hero had trouble staying on his horse as the cow charged him. He soon had her lassoed – and the rope broke. A second rope held and the cow was held between two horses. I got the radio call to go pick her up. And I missed catching any of it on film.

It took quite a while to persuade her to get into the trailer. It seems she'd lost her calf at birth and we wondered if she thought it was still back in the pasture. Who knows what animals think. However, we all knew her behavior won her a quick trip to the Winnipeg Cattle Auction!

I wasn't keen on driving with a "mad" cow, so I drove to catch up to Bob to trade riding and driving. He'd galloped steady for six miles and the horse wouldn't stand still long enough for him to get off so that I could get on. He rode. I drove.

The rest of the journey continued without incident. The rocking motion of the trailer seemed to quiet my passenger and I delivered her safely to the corral. I arrived slightly ahead of the herd and welcomed them all as they straggled in. *And I finally caught it on film.* The outriders were dirty and tired, but broad smiles creased every face. Laughter rang out as they regaled each other with the retelling of the stampede and the rogue cow. A modern day roundup it was, but with all the camaraderie of the roundups of long ago!

Joan McCallister

Biography - Joan McCallister operates a grain/cattle farm with her husband and three children in southern Manitoba. The family owns five horses and her daughter, Katie, continues a family tradition of 4-H and horses. Active in several organizations, Joan co-edited the Around the Kitchen Table books for the Manitoba Farm Women's Conference. The stories, of farm adventures and misadventures, have been enjoyed by farm lovers everywhere. Around the Kitchen Table – a 2nd Harvest is available for $15 (postage & handling included) c/o J. McCallister, RR1 Box 68, Portage La Prairie, Manitoba, Canada, R1N 3A1 or phone: 1-204-857-8092.

The Perfect Pony

I was doing cartwheels across the living room floor and whooping like a Comanche child when I was told that Smokey Jett Jr., the Icelandic pony I had been caring for and riding, was my birthday present. I immediately ran outside and hugged his shaggy neck and planted an enthusiastic six-year-old's kiss upon his clover-scented velvet muzzle. I had been so disconsolate when my first pony was sold, but here it was, less than a year later, and I had my second pony.

Smokey was a city-dwelling backyard pony now; it had certainly been a long haul from the barren beauty of Iceland, a continent and an ocean away. Smokey, whose registered name I have since forgotten, was imported from Iceland in the early 1960's and made his way across most of the U.S. before finally becoming a little girl's very best friend in Tarzana, California. .

Smokey was tiny, but always looked and "rode" big because of his near-perfect conformation. He was black in the summer, brown in the winter and mustard yellow in the spring and fall: it was like having three different ponies each year. Smokey had double diamonds on his face - a very large one between his eyes, and a miniature twin to it between his nostrils - which were shaped like perfect 9's. I have always thought of those markings as symbols of his pricelessness. He had an extremely shaggy hair coat in the wintertime (we used to call him "Buffalo-Boy"), but his furry fetlocks and abundant mane stayed as they were year-round, always attracting lots of compliments. His forelock looked just like a big powder puff and it always seemed to be sitting poised at attention over his kind, dark-chocolate eyes. Smokey's eyes were always soft and infinitely wise: never rimmed in white or tightened in anger.

It didn't matter to me that Smokey was imported, nor that he was one of a rare and wonderful breed – only that, unlike Cinnamon, my first pony, he loved me and took care of me... and put up with me. Poor Smokey had to wear birthday hats, groom's outfits (he got married more often than Mickey Rooney), silly outfits of various style and fashion, and even a glittered, styrofoam unicorn horn one Halloween. He accepted my "dress up" phase with his usual quiet dignity, and even gave the cats and pet rats rides on his back at my behest (not at the same time, though - even the long-suffering Smokey would have drawn the line there, I think).

More than just a riding horse, Smokey was always a part of the family. He was brought inside the house at the slightest whim, but Thanksgiving (he loved the stuffing) and Yule were always special occasions, during which he would delight our friends and family with his quiet manner and gentle disposition, "sitting around" with the rest of us. None of the neighborhood kids could ever believe my mom would let me bring a horse inside the house. Not only did she let me, she was often the instigator. She liked to show her friends how he could lap champagne from a glass and clean up any leftovers. He obliged her with his usual aplomb, then accepted pats and ear-rubs from everyone present.

As with most ponies, the way to Smokey's heart was undoubtedly through his stomach. He loved anything humans ate. Among his favorites were soda, which he could drink from a can or a bottle, pizza, French fries, corn chips, corn-on-the cob, and especially candy of all sorts (his favorite was Snickers). I'll never forget the look of his little black bewhiskered muzzle, lips extended and reaching much like the tip of an elephant's trunk for his treat. He was always very careful and never once bit anybody.

Over the next couple of years, Smokey and I competed in many horse shows. I loved it, while he merely tolerated it. He never won a trophy, but with each ribbon that was pinned to his bridle he became the Champion of the World to me. Of course, we did come away with nothing often, too; like when Smokey decided it was time for a good roll in the middle of the show ring, or when he made a bee-line to my mom at the arena rail, hoping to score a treat. Perhaps the most embarrassing moment was when he drooled on the judge's beautiful Australian lizard-skin cowboy boots.

As safe, calm, gentle and well-trained as Smokey was, it was rides on Smokey that led to my most serious falls and injuries as a beginner rider. I'm the first to admit it was almost always my fault: I took advantage of Smokey's excellent disposition and willingness, and being young and bold, often asked him to take jumps that were too high or to do things that were really quite dangerous. It was always me who always ended up with the concussion, whiplash, broken leg, various cuts, scrapes, bruises, lacerations and contusions. Smokey never even turned a hair during any of those "accidents"!

Even though I must admit I put Smokey into jeopardy many times with my foolishness, he always took only the best care of me. I remember the first winter we lived in Idyllwild, a lovely resort town in the mountains of Southern California. It had snowed heavily that year, heavier than many of the lifelong residents could ever remember. Smokey was right in his element, probably for the first time since he'd lived in Iceland as a young colt. I had an Appaloosa mare as well then, and while she stood shivering under a blanket in the barn, Smokey would be outside in the thick of things, letting the snow pile up several inches deep on his back. At first I took him back into the barn, only to find an hour or so later that he had found another way to escape back to the windswept pasture. One time I felt beneath the snow on his withers, just to see how wet and cold he was, only to find his skin completely dry and actually very warm. I later learned that Icelandics have a special hair coat that allows this natural insulation to take place. Smokey always knew best, and from that day forth I never argued with him about staying in the barn.

One sunny but crisp day in February, after an intense week-long snow-storm, I decided to take Smokey out for a ride. I had a severe case of cabin fever and I suspect Smokey did too, because as I groomed and bridled him he acted as though he couldn't wait to get out. The tiny fellow was practically buried alive by the many snowdrifts that had accumulated just in our driveway on the way out, but he was un-daunted. He just chugged along like a little snowmobile. We went up the ploughed street, Smokey's little iron gray hooves slipping ever-so-slightly on the thin coat of ice. Finally we made it onto the bridle trail. An uncharted white world lay stretched out before us: no one apparently had ridden since the last snow. We knew the trails near home well and, under a breathtaking canopy of towering firs and oaks, serenaded by the songs of birds and the chatter of gray squirrels, we made our way well into the mountains.

I decided that I wanted to cut across an unfamiliar meadow, then loop down to the hiking trail that passed Tahquitz Peak and head for home. Smokey entered the snow-blanketed meadow quite will-ingly at first, but then he suddenly stopped dead and wouldn't budge. I tried circling him. I tried coaxing him. I tried backing him in the direction I had chosen. I tried threatening him with talk of how glue is made. Nothing worked. I even got off and tried to lead him. It was like trying to move the Rock of Gibraltar. Defeated by an 11.2-hand -high pony with (I hate to say it) a brain the size of a walnut, I turned and headed him back the way we had come.

It wasn't for another two months, after the spring thaw, that I rode that particular trail again. As I entered the meadow clearing, the first thing I saw was the sun sparkling off a big, beautiful pond - a pond that had laid directly in the path I had tried to force Smokey to take on that snowy February day. Had he done as I commanded, we could have found ourselves on thin ice in a world of trouble with no one for miles around. People say that equines aren't smart and that they don't have the capacity for affection, but that one event crys-tallizes in my mind the intelligence of that special pony, and the love he must have felt for "his" little girl.

Smokey was always there for me, especially when as a teenager I went through the usual emotional turmoil. I would lay my cheek against his bushy roached mane and cry softly into his neck, telling him he was the only friend in the world who understood me. And he did. Sympathetically, he would nudge me with his muzzle and "tell" me everything was going be okay. Smokey was a teenager too by this time, but he never showed any signs of his age.

In later years, after I was married and began my career, Smokey was still a major part of my life. Although time had grayed his muzzle and taken away some of his good health, Smokey was still full of vim and vigor and enjoyed rides out.

One sunny August day, I decided to take him out for a hack alone. It was a beautiful afternoon, and I could think of no one better to share the sunset with. Now living on the California coast, Smokey and I made our way to the best lookout point jutting over the Pacific ocean.

As when we were younger, I imagined that Smokey was a combination between the Black Stallion and Seattle Slew as he pulled eagerly against the bridle, waiting to be unleashed. I let him go up the trail that led to the point and he soared like an eagle, his little iron gray hooves beating the ground for a split second before he was airborne again, galloping like a wild mustang. The wind whipped my hair and whistled in my ears; I leaned forward, my legs warm against his bare back, my face close to his neck. The sunset hit at about seven-thirty, splashing the pale blue sky with deep red, gold and lavender. I remember leaning back on Smokey's rump, letting my reins go in ultimate trust, and lying with my back against his to gaze at the sky until the moon came up.

At the time, I didn't know I would never ride my beloved pony again. Smokey passed away peacefully three days later. That was in 1988, and I still miss his sweet face and kind soul every day.

Staci Layne Wilson

Biography - Staci Layne Wilson is the author of The Horse's Choice (training how-to) and The Dance (horsy fiction). "I've loved horses ever since I could formulate the words to start asking my mom for one. I've worked as a trainer, and as a writer for publications such as Horse Illustrated and Horse and Horseman. Right now I am down to just one horse, a fuzzy Palomino Icelandic named Faxi, who looks (and acts!) just like the Thelwell Pony." You can visit Staci on the web at http://www.staciwilson.com.

A Trainer In Training

At the end of my 12ᵗʰ year, I had saved enough money to purchase my first pony. With the help of my riding instructor, we found a large middle-aged Pinto pony. While he had a fancy name of his own, given to him by my father, I simply called him "Berny." He was easy going, did everything I asked him to do and on the day we took him for a test ride, the three children of the owner were standing on his back doing circus tricks as Berny plodded quietly around the paddock.

I had spent the past four years taking riding lessons, mucking stalls, riding sale horses and exercising a string of wild polo ponies. To have my own pony was as good as it gets. I had watched the trainers at my barn working with all the fancy show horses each week. These horses were high strung and easily spooked but the trainers were patient and determined to work through their fears. Inspired by those trainers, I decided that I would train Berny just like they trained all those fancy show horses.

I asked my riding instructor what was the hardest thing to teach a horse to do? He told me that most horses don't like water and for most horse owners, that is the toughest hurdle. I thought, right then, water it is. I will teach Berny not to be afraid of water and I will use all the same techniques that the trainers were using on the fancy show horses. So, one fine summer day, after giving Berny a thorough work out, I headed down to the man-made lake behind the barn. I had a big plan and was determined to succeed.

I had worked him thoroughly so he wouldn't be so proned to give me a hard time. He was sweaty so the water would probably feel good to him, provided I could get him within a block of it and I was completely prepared with my three-foot-long lead line and all the patience in the world.

We headed out alone to the lake because I didn't want any distractions. We were going to succeed and I didn't want anyone to spook my horse during our training session. After all those fancy show horses were always spooking at something and if they were that bad, I could only imagine what I was in for since Berny was neither fancy, nor a show horse.

I was surprised that Berny followed me faithfully towards the lake. He could see the water and didn't hesitate. I thought I was the best trainer in the world at that moment, until Berny kept walking past me and headed straight into the lake, dragging me at the end of that three foot lead line screaming "WHOA" at the top of my lungs. Undaunted by my screams, Berny proceeded to repeatedly stomp the water with his front hoof, getting us both soaked in the process. I jerked on that lead line for all I was worth but Berny wasn't budging. He was going to have a beautiful roll in that luscious water with or without me. I was knee deep in the lake hanging on for dear life until Berny finished his dip. Afterwards, he happily followed me out of the lake and shook off like a spin cycle in a washing machine, soaking me from head to toe. At 12-years-old, how was I supposed to know that there were actually horses in the world that were not afraid of water? It never dawned on me that any horse might like water. I was boarding in a show barn where everything was afraid of water.

I led him back to the barn hoping that we could sneak in without being noticed. Unfortunately, I was met at the door by one of the girls who owned one of those fancy show horses. "What in the world happened to you?" She asked. "I took Berny down to the lake and he decided to go for a swim." I said in a mortified tone. "Wow are you lucky to have a horse that isn't afraid of water. I wish my horse would do that." The show horse owner said. "But your horse is so fancy and Berny... is just Berny." I said. "I would give all the money in the world for a horse that I could trust like that." She said. "Do you have any idea how hard it is to ride a horse that spooks all the time? A horse that you can't trust is the worst. You are really lucky to have a horse like Berny." With that she patted him on his soaking wet neck.

As I removed the excess water from his coat in the aisle, I thought to myself, "Berny you might not be as fancy looking as those show horses, but you are certainly the bravest horse in this barn.

In retrospect, I wonder how any horse survives life with a 12-year-old rider. While I was busy trying to "train" Berny, I see now who was actually doing the training and who just thought they were!

Bonnie Marlewski-Probert

Biography - Bonnie Marlewski-Probert is a professionally trained horseman with 20 years of safe, responsible teaching and training experience. She has published more than 1000 magazine articles, several books and videos for horse lovers around the world. To learn more about Bonnie's work, visit her web site at TheCompletePet.com. To order books, call 800-700-5096 or order via the web site.

Saying Good-Bye
Chapter Six

Partners

A Horseman's Prayer

Tonight as I lie on my bedroll,
And stare at the stars in the sky,
I can't help but think of my partners,
The critters I've had to watch die.

Sometimes was a bullet that claimed them,
Or a needle in a kind horse doc's hand.
But whatever was used,
They were never abused,
Just sent on ahead to God's land.

Andy, my son's Palomino,
Lies buried on a hillside so green.
And faithful old Dan,
Who grew too weak to stand,
Is interred in a place most serene.

Buck and the Arab called Randy
Lie near Dan beneath the sod.
My friend and his wife,
Who loved them in life,
Are committed now, too, to our God.

Saying Good-bye

Gypsy is buried in Texas.
I sold her and her foal to a friend.
How could I know
That she'd come to woe,
And colic so bad in the end?

There's even a Collie named Laddie,
And a dog that we called Smokey Bear.
We loved them for years,
They left with our tears,
And we trusted them, too, to God's care.

There's Spider, and Bear Dog, my wife loved,
And Big Jake, the best of them all.
The longer the list,
The more they are missed,
I wish they could come when I call.

My old Appaloosa named Steamy,
Most recently left us behind.
Cancer beset him,
We'll never forget him,
Or the young vet whose treatment was kind.

Lord, I know that You're up there in heaven.
And I pray that my pals are there, too.
They served me so well,
My life would have been hell,
If I'd lived it without them and You.

When I come to the end of my journey,
And my time on this planet is done,
Your pastures so real,
And your waters so still,
Will be waiting when my race is run.

Saying Good-bye

If my partners are waiting to greet me,
I'll know I'm in heaven for sure.
Lord, it's Your creatures below,
That loved their master so,
Who taught me of love that is pure.

So Master of mine, up in heaven,
Look down on this rider tonight.
Forgive all his sins,
And bless all his friends,
And keep him safe till your morning light.

Ted W. Land

Biography - Ted W. Land. A Presbyterian minister since 1971, Ted Land has been pastor of First Presbyterian Church in Arcadia, Florida since 1985. Arcadia is a "cow town". Gooseneck trailers with saddled horses resting in them are common sights on the parking lots of restaurants in Arcadia. Ted Land has served as a director of the All Florida Championship Rodeo and President of the All Florida Saddle Club. Born in 1946 in Knoxville, Tennessee, Ted Land learned to ride Tennessee Walkers. He has written extensively about Walking Horses, but his favorite mount remains an Appaloosa.

The Horse Of My Dreams

In October, 1993, I went looking for the horse of my dreams. I already had a great horse named Snazzy, but she had been diagnosed with navicular several years earlier. After surgery and various other treatments, the fact remained that I couldn't ride Snazzy the way I wanted to ride without causing her pain. So, while Snazzy began her retirement, becoming the matriarch of the pasture, I began my search.

I lucked out right away, or so I thought, when I found a striking blue roan gelding off the Navaho Indian Reservation. I purchased him from a woman who was a horse trader and needless to say, it turned out to be a disaster. After one broken arm and a severe concussion, I called the lady and insisted she take him back. After yet another bad trade, she finally admitted that the only other horse she had was a small, sickly gelding named Pawnee Bill. He, too, was off the Navaho Indian Reservation and was a half-brother to the first horse we tried. We changed his name to Indian Bill Davidson, due to his brand, "IBD", and my last name, Davidson.

I fell in love immediately, and the feeling grew every time I rode him. He would go anywhere I asked and do anything I wanted him to do. I finally had the horse I had always wanted. As my husband said, he would climb straight up the wall if I asked him to.

Then it happened. In the summer of 1996, I was riding in the Estrella Mountains with my friend, Gayle Smith. She noticed a lump on the left side of Bill's withers. At first the vets just thought it was an abscess, but Bill was eventually diagnosed with fistulous withers.

122

He went through many, many smaller procedures and eventually a major surgery. The incision was 18 inches long. Every day the area had to be scrubbed, flushed out and new medicine administered. Even though he was on very strong pain medication, Bill would cringe but still stand quietly every time I had to do this.

Finally on July 2nd, 1997, Bill was put down. A full year had passed since the discovery of his illness and this boy could take no more. He was hundreds of pounds lighter and the spirit was gone from his eyes.

The last day, Bill got every treat in the world - all those things I didn't give him before because I didn't want to upset his stomach. It wouldn't matter now.

I knew the vet, Dr. Kloppe, was concerned when he arrived that morning, as I was the only one home. My husband, Jay, offered to stay behind, but I said no. My girlfriend, Gayle, offered to be there, but I said no. I knew I wouldn't be able to be strong for Bill if they were there.

So it was just Dr. Kloppe, Bill and I. He was such a good guy right to the end. I talked to him and petted him. It went very quickly.

A good friend of mine, Mike, had assisted us in preparing a grave for Bill, so I was able to bury him at home in his own pasture. Gayle Smith had planned to come out on her lunch hour, whether I wanted her to or not. She brought a yellow rose, which we put in Bill's grave with him, and this poem. She wrote it in the middle of the night when her heart was breaking for me:

Hoof Prints

A heavy heart, a tender rose
In the wind his forelock blows,
As it whispers, you will know
It was time for him to go.

Saying Good-bye

Tears flowing down your face
He'll be made perfect in God's grace.
Now memories of "IBD"
Will live on in you and me,
Leaving empty space you'll never fill
Nothing can take the place of Bill

A friend like one you've never known,
Through his weakness you have grown.
The bond that ties you, now complete,
As he lay peaceful at your feet.

A trusting friend from the start,
Carving hoof prints on your heart.

If I were asked which horse I would spend eternity with, I would
say Bill is waiting for me in the pasture.

Su Davidson

Biography - Su Davidson. "I live in Arizona, where I have been a police of-
ficer for 19 and a half years. I am married, have three children, three dogs, a
cat, a rabbit, and five horses. I will be retiring in the next few months and hope
to do some training and lessons."

Forever, Little Bit

The poem I am going to share with you was written about my youngest daughter, who was given a pony when she was young. In all my
years of teaching, I have never again seen the special bond that
those two had. I am convinced that children, horses and ponies are
a gift from above, for all of us to learn from.

How do you describe Forever?
For when you are young, everything is Forever.
Forever is when you look into the eyes of your pony
who looks back with eyes for you only.
Forever is that soft touch of her nose when she
nuzzles close to you
Forever is how you call her name and her whinny is
only understood by you.
Forever is how you remember all her markings as if
you drew them yourself.

And when we grow up some, Forever takes on a new
renewed meaning...
Like Forever, you will remember how much fun it was
to teach your pony to jump... Oh Boy and
that water jump...
Forever will it be that you remember those dressage
tests... The ones in the ring and the ones
out of the ring...
Forever will you remember playing hide and seek.

And Forever will you feel the cool air on your face
and your pony beneath you, galloping like
the wind...beating the socks off the horses!
Forever is the memory of your pony dressing up for
Halloween and how you shared your candy –

Saying Good-bye
you eating your favorites and your pony
enjoying the "other stuff."

And when we grew too big, Forever meant
"Driving Miss Daisy" around in her little
black cart.
Forever meant that what you and your pony learned
could now help others to learn
Forever now seemed to be long walks and private talks,

It seemed that Forever meant a way of sharing between
two close friends, as comfortable as the
clothes they wore.
Forever was taking care of each other, no matter what.

Forever was never meant to end, never meant to be
final or to have your heart broken.

Forever now is standing alone, an empty spot beside
you, nothing to touch, a moment with no
one to share it with.
Feeling older, now Forever takes on a new meaning.

Forever is what you keep deep within your heart now,
a kind of gift to open when you feel alone.
Forever is the smile on your face, a warm glow in
your eyes and a heart full of the gifts that
make memories to be unwrapped, enjoyed and
savored with each Little Bit.

Sandi Every

Biography - Sandi lives on Cape Cod with her husband Tom, their two daughters Tanya and Tara, and the family pets, Java the lab, Patty the cat, and two horses, Bailey and Knicker. When not being a private caregiver, she enjoys teaching horseback riding at Sea Horse Farm in Harwich, Mass., and being able to ride and compete herself. Sandi volunteers once a week for a local Outreach Program and is treasurer for the Cape Cod Dressage Association. She is a freelance writer and has written poetry reflecting her interesting life experiences with family, friends, students and horses. She can be reached at her e-mail address: JAVA2@prodigy.com

Saying Good-bye

Saying good-bye is something I often thought of, but hoped would never happen. Unfortunately, I had to say good-bye recently to the most wonderful horse. Her name was Lady Bug; she was my first horse. I got her when I was 12 and I grew up with her. She was my teacher and my best friend for the past 18 years. As time went by, Lady began to show her age, but it was not until recently that she became quite ill.

I had the first vet out in the middle of March, as Lady was having trouble walking and was not eating (which was so unlike her). He decided to try her on bute for a week. After a week, things did not get better; in fact, they got worse.

One morning, Lady did not eat breakfast, but instead went outside to graze. I went back to bed and woke up at noon. When I got up, I found her down on her side, unwilling to get up. I quickly called the vet and got the on-call vet, with whom I was not familiar. I said to her, "I think my horse has laid down to die - please come quickly!"

When the vet arrived, Lady remained down even after a dose of Banamine. I felt it was over at that point, as I didn't feel she had any more fight in her. Then the vet said, "Boy, this old girl doesn't want to quit." After she said that, I gave her the okay to do what was necessary to save my horse.

We got Lady up and she began to walk, but it was very painful for her. The conclusion was that she might be dehydrated, as well as having some colic due to poor water intake and stress. That night, we put her on IV therapy and kept her on pain medication three

127

times a day. She slowly seemed to get some light back in her eyes, but it would only be for brief periods. She began to eat some bran mashes, but still would not drink.

After day two of IVs, things still were not going well. The vet started coming out twice a day to tube her with mineral oil and water. The next day, the obstruction seemed to pass, but then she started going downhill again. She kept looking at her side. Her heart rate would increase and her bowel sounds would decrease. What was wrong with my mare? Why did the colic not get better, or cause a rupture?

Then we tried ulcer medicine and her appetite improved for a few days and she began to drink. I was so happy when I thought she was on the road to recovery; unfortunately, she was not. It was false hope and denial; I knew we were losing her. Five days after her last treatment, I called the vets and asked them what they rec-ommended we do – I did not want her to suffer. What I was looking for was someone to tell me it was time. However, the vets would not make this decision for me - it was a decision I had to make.

I called an old friend and explained to him what was going on. He gave me the answer I needed to hear. He told me I needed to let her go with some dignity and that it was her time, as she was in pain and too old for any surgery. I then called the vet and said it was time to put her to sleep, but I needed another day to say good-bye. She agreed and told me that since the colic was neither getting bet-ter or worse, and given that her physical exam showed some cancer cells in her eye and on her back, it may be possible that she had a tumor causing the obstruction. But at 27, she did not recommend surgery.

The next day arrived; I had changed my mind several times through the night. I kept asking myself - is this what she would want? Am I doing the right thing? I called the vet at 11:00 a.m. and asked if I could change the time from 2:00 p.m. until 4:00 p.m., because I needed more time.

Saying Good-bye

I decided to give Lady some time with her two buddies that she had been with for years. I put them in a separate pasture together. I could tell that the other horses knew she was ill. They would all yell to her and look at her all day long through the barn window.

Lady began to graze with her pals while I took pictures and cleaned stalls. At 1:50 p.m. I went to check on the horses and saw Lady was down. I ran down the hill, crying as I thought she passed away, but at the same time felt relief that she had passed on her own. She was alive – she lifted her head when she heard me running. I lay by her side and rubbed her head and told her it was okay to let go. She did not have to suffer anymore. She started to twitch, shake and gasp. I debated whether I should run up the hill to the barn and get the phone to call the vet, or stay by her side to let her know I was there for her. After a while, I made the decision to call the vet, because I thought she was suffering. When I was coming back down the hill one of her buddies, Mike, came up and bit her, like he was saying, "get up, don't give up." She squealed and got to her feet. I was upset, but I now know that Mike was mourning her and it was his way of keeping her around.

At 2:30 p.m., the vet arrived. Now I lost it - it was really going to happen. I wanted to tell the vet to go away, but I knew this had to be done. As she entered the field, all the horses went crazy and started running around, looking at Lady. The vet gave Lady a sedative as I stood there looking into her eyes and telling her how sorry I was. The vet said the other horses were upset and that it would be a good idea to bring them to see her after it was over so that they would know she was gone. She said, "I'm going to give her two shots then I want you to step back and give her to me." I couldn't believe this was happening. I just kept crying and shaking – I wanted to say *stop*!

Then it was done. My baby was lying there. I hugged her as I wept over her for the next hour. Did I do the right thing? The question keeps haunting me.

I did as the vet mentioned and brought Mike and Noel down to say good-bye. I would not have believed it if I did not see it for myself. Mike went up to her and the first thing he did was bite her; when she did not react, he did it again. Still not having a reaction, he went to her face and began to pull on her ear. When he saw none of this was working, he put his nose to hers for a few minutes, and then took off at a gallop. Noel also touched noses with her and then took off running. It broke my heart to watch them say good-bye.

The next morning, I could not get out of bed. I did not want to go to the barn and see her empty stall. My husband fed the horses and we turned them out in a paddock where they could not see Lady. The horses again went nuts, running around and screaming for her. I came out and brought them all down to see her again and then kept them in for the day. They continued to call for her; it hurt so badly to watch them listen for a response.

We buried her that afternoon. When the time came, I lost it again. I did not want to let go. I could not stand the thought of never seeing her, or touching her soft velvet nose. I held onto her and said some more good-byes. When it was time, I buried her with a letter apologizing for my decision and telling her how much I will love and miss her, two silk roses, one from me and one from my husband, and a lock of my hair, as I took a lock of hers. I told her we would meet at Rainbow Bridge.

It has only been a week now and things are still hard – like typing this story. March 31st would have marked our 18th year together.

It is during times like this that you discover who your friends are. I want to extend my thanks to the two vets, Linda and Stacy of Equine Care, that were so kind and helpful. I thank you with all my heart for your kindness and your caring nature, for being at my house at all hours of the day and night, and for always returning my calls. Thank you to my dad for being there and taking care of the burial, and to all my family, as they will also miss her. And thank you to my friend, Ray, for telling me the words most people do not want to hear - but need to.

Saying good-bye is never easy, but I can go to sleep at night knowing she is no longer in pain and hoping she is in heaven doing the two things she loved most - running and eating!

Sherri L. Pasquale

Biography - Sherri L. Pasquale. "I have been riding since I was six-years-old. My grandfather bought me my first horse, Lady Bug, when I was 11. I'm 30 and live with my husband Maurizio on our small farm. We currently have four horses, a pony, two goats, three pigs, two sheep, three cats and five dogs. You may be able to tell my hobby is collecting and saving the unwanted. I am a registered nurse in the emergency room at our local hospital."

Raindrop Will

I was about to graduate from high school in a month, and I already had the next four years of my life planned out perfectly. I was going to go to college, get on the rodeo team, receive a full ride scholarship and everything else would just fall into place.

"Come on mom. Let's go! We need to get on the road now!" I screamed out across the freshly mowed yard. This weekend was already starting out badly. My sister had just plowed her car into the back end of my horse trailer, bending the hitch on my one-week-old truck. I quickly checked the damage, decided everything would work just fine for now, got in my truck and hit the road.

It took about 30 minutes to get to the farm where I boarded my horse, Raindrop. Her full name is Raindrop Will, because she was born in a thunderstorm and she would do anything for me. She is a gorgeous 18-year-old dark bay Appendix Quarter Horse. Even though she is up there in years, she can run like the wind.

I was a bit concerned, because for the past two days her left hind leg was slightly swollen, probably from running her hard, but it looked much better today. Within the next ten minutes, we had loaded all of my stuff, and my mother and I were back on the road with Raindrop, heading south for yet another rodeo.

When I pulled into the rodeo grounds, I unloaded my horse and then waited for the rodeo to get underway. Raindrop ran really well that night; we were second in the pole bending and were scheduled to run goats and barrels on Sunday morning with the slack. My mother and I were confident that I was going to have a good weekend.

Sunday morning seemed to roll around way too fast for me, and I had to run slack at 10 a.m. Raindrop wasn't running as well as she had the night before, but we did well enough, anyway. The second go for the weekend was going to start at 2 p.m., so we had about an hour and a half to wait. I put Raindrop away so that she could rest and I could take a nap, but I really don't think that either one of us got any rest in that 90-minute time period.

At two o'clock, I got Raindrop ready for the grand entry, where everyone rides into the ring carrying flags in a pattern, following the Rodeo Queen. We entered about fifth from the end, and it was so incredibly dry and dusty that it was hard to really see anything. As we were about three-quarters of the way through the pattern, I could feel Raindrop cantering strangely. She usually felt smooth and comfortable, like a Lazy Boy recliner, but she suddenly felt more like a broken rocking horse. Raindrop didn't want to stop, so I let her keep going.

As we were exiting the ring, a man started yelling, "Hey, your horse is on three legs. Get off! Get off your horse!" I was so confused. All of these people started to gather around me. I quickly jumped off to see what he was talking about. Sure enough, she was on three legs-her right rear was in the air. Within minutes, I had received at least ten different opinions as to what was wrong and what I should do. People told me everything from a pulled muscle to torn ligaments and even a simple muscle spasm was the problem. I didn't know what to think.

A vet on the grounds advised us to take her back to the trailer, call another vet and ice her leg while we waited. My mother and I did just that. About five hours later, we finally got a vet to come out to the grounds to check out my horse. He was really very nice to us and advised us to haul her back home, since he did not have the right equipment to perform x-rays. He diagnosed her with either a torn ligament, tendon damage or a possible bone fracture. I was devastated; my dreams were being washed away as I watched my horse hobble around, but I didn't lose hope.

The vet wrapped Raindrop's leg and helped us load her into the trailer. He advised us to call another vet in the morning and have x-rays taken. We thanked him for coming out and started down the road at about 9:30 p.m. We finally arrived back at Blue Lakes around 1:00 a.m. Monday morning, and tried to make Raindrop as comfortable as possible for the night, then we headed for home ourselves.

At about 9:00 a.m. I called my veterinarian and told her what had happened and that x-rays were needed. She came out to the farm and took about five x-rays of Raindrop's leg and told us she would have the results that afternoon. She also told us that things were not good. "Kris, I don't know how to tell you this," she said. "Raindrop definitely has a hairline fracture, possibly even a broken pastern bone. It's fixable, but it will be expensive." If this was true, the only way to repair her leg would be through surgery, and both my mother and I knew that we could not afford it.

So we sat and waited for the results. What seemed like an eternity was only about four hours, and when the vet finally called us she had bad news: all of her x-rays jammed, and her machine was broken down. She advised us to get hold of any vet that could take x-rays at the farm and to do it as soon as possible.

We called about three or four different vets before finding someone who could come out and take some x-rays. A vet from the Aurora Veterinarian Hospital finally arrived, took about six x-rays and told us he would call within the hour. At about 4:30 p.m., the vet called us and gave us the worst news of my life; Raindrop had a broken pastern, a fracture coming off of the break and a few pieces of bone floating around. I was nearly hysterical. I wrapped my arms around Raindrop's neck and just kept crying.

We had two choices. We could put her to sleep or we could have surgery done to fix the bone. Everyone at the barn knew that we could not afford the surgery, even though she had a very good chance of coming back 100 per cent. I told my mother we were going to have to put her down, but she assured me that we would be able to save my horse. I trusted in her judgement and decided that somehow we could make the surgery possible.

Once again, we loaded Raindrop in the trailer and took her to the veterinary hospital. They were going to perform the surgery the next morning. I cried all the way home when we left her there. After the surgery, we found out that everything went well, but Raindrop's chances of a full recovery were very slim now. When the vets operated, the damage to her leg was much greater than the x-rays had revealed. At this point, she was probably going to be a pasture horse and possibly never ridden again. I didn't lose hope; I knew that my horse was going to get better, and I would rodeo with her again. I went to see her every day, even though I hated being at the hospital.

Within the next few days, Raindrop's progress was so good that the vets took her off the painkillers so that she would not move around so much. I felt very confident that she was going to make it all the way back to normal. I kept visiting her every day, brushing her, talking to her and feeding her carrots. The vets were surprised by her progress and told me that anything could happen. Raindrop was a real fighter.

Then we got the call on Wednesday morning, nearly two weeks after Raindrop had broken her pastern bone at the rodeo. The vets had been doing check-up x-rays when they discovered that another bone underneath the one they fixed had collapsed. We were given three options: surgery again, let it heal by itself, or put her to sleep. We could not do the surgery again because of the expense and she only had a 20 per cent chance of walking. We decided to let her stand on it and see if it would heal by itself, since it was already in a cast. Four days later, the vet called and told us that she was in a great deal of pain and we either needed to do the surgery or put her to sleep.

135

We decided that we would bring her home the next night and bury her at our family farm. Monday came so incredibly fast for me. I did not want to go and pick up my horse. We arrived at the vet hospital late that evening and loaded Raindrop. It was the hardest thing that I have ever had to do. I tried so hard not to cry, but the tears just kept flowing. I could barely see where I was driving my mom was crying, too.

As we pulled into the drive of our farm, I saw my dad standing there and I lost it. I was barely able to breathe. We drove my horse into the back field and parked the truck. I did not want to unload her, but I knew that I had to because it was better for her. My family and I just stood there in the pasture with her for a few minutes as she ate grass. I gave her one last, long hug and a carrot. I'll always remember that she spit out that carrot and just gave me this heart-breaking look. It seemed like she knew what was going to happen, and was grateful that I had made the right choice for her.

I had to walk away at that point and get back into my truck. My future seemed a mess; all of my plans, hopes and dreams were crushed when I drove away from Raindrop. To this day, I still go to where she is buried and sit and talk to her. I realized through this experience that I can't plan my life out - God deals all of the cards and all I can do is hold them.

Kris Robison

Biography - Kris Robison. "Raised on a registered Jersey dairy farm in Thompson, Ohio, I became involved with horses when I was eight. Thanks to my trainer of six years, Kim McElroy, I am the horsewoman that I am today. I currently live in Bozeman, Montana, and attend Montana State University in pursuit of a B.S. in Animal Science with a minor in Agricultural Business. I own a two-year-old Palomino Quarter Horse mare that is my first project since I lost Raindrop. I'd like to thank my family, especially my mom Mary Jane and Adam, for their support of my horse habit."

Horses Will Be Horses!
The Door

In the fall of 1905, my dad came west from Quebec on a harvest excursion train. He got off at Griswold Manitoba and was hired the same day on a steam outfit. After this job was finished, he went back east, did a lot of thinking about his future, decided that he liked what he had seen of the farming and the people in Manitoba. Early 1905 found him in Portage la Prairie quite decided to learn farming western style.

In the fall of 1906 he was hired by Mr. Thomas Wishart, whose homestead was a short distance north of Portage on what was then called the town line, now #240. He was to do chores for the winter months. Doing chores meant doing a wide range of different jobs, including getting wood sawed (sawing bees were near spring), then splitting and piling it to dry during the summer. He hauled hay, feed, straw, and manure by horse team only, thawed frozen pumps with a kettle of boiling water, etc., etc., etc.

I was quite young when he told me the following true story. Evening chore time was just about dark and very frosty. This evening the horses, a sizable herd, were milling around waiting for the barn door to open to let them get in to their evening feed and shelter. Now anyone that knows anything at all about a horse knows there's always one that does or sees something that can add a bit of excitement to hurry things up a bit. This horse in particular noticed an old five-panel door, one panel missing, leaning up against a shed. Naturally it called for immediate investigation. Going up closer to see, he decided to put his head through, probably to see what color the door was painted. Instantaneously he realized he was in trouble, he threw his head up quickly and the door settled nicely over his neck, kitty cornered. Now things really started to go haywire, he ran towards the others, knees banging the door with every leap. For the horses to see a door with a horse's head in it, and moving, was a bit too much. As one they all went through the gate, as though there had never been one, and ran out onto the road. Turning north they were off and running, with old "head in the door" trailing front knees pounding on the door as though he were playing the drums for them.

It wasn't a decision to jump in a vehicle and chase them, it was strictly sleight roads, so the men decided to go in and have some supper and think.

In the barn was one horse, probably the school pony or a driver, so with a lantern, pony, and cutter, away they went after supper. The tracking was easy.

After a few miles they came upon old "head in the door". They freed him of the cross he was carrying and other than bleeding legs and neck he was none the worse, but maybe a bit wiser.

After several more miles the tracks turned into a gateless lane and standing in a group, soaking wet, steaming heavily and turning white with frost, the lost were found and ready to go home.

My dad, he was Lester Mason. He later bought a quarter section in Oakland in 1911. In 1915 he married my mother. I was the eldest of six children.

Annie Cuthbert

Biography -AnnieCuthbert. Born in 1916, the eldest of six children, Annie had a wonderful opportunity right from the start to get acquainted with horses as they were the source of power on the farm. She had a school pony for the three miles to school and during harvest she drove the grain team. After marrying a farmer, she raised Shetland and Welsh cross ponies. The last one lived to be 40-years-old. She and her husband are still in the country with family nearby. She has very happy memories of the animals she was fortunate to know.

138

New Beginnings
Chapter Seven

J.J.

Author's note: *This is the first story I have ever attempted to get published. If this makes it into the book, it is meant as a thank-you to all who have helped me succeed in the horse world and for teaching me all I need to know: my mom, who wanted this horse for me as much as I wanted it (and for so many other reasons); my dad for saying yes and being the best dad there ever was (he's finally adapting to the whole horse thing). Thank you to all those special people. You know who you are.* -Alissa Ricci

"Oh, man, I can't wait until next week," said my riding instructor, the infamous Becky. She had a strange look on her face, like she had some big secret that she just could not wait to reveal. This only baited my curiosity.

"Why, what is going to happen?" I asked, knowing that Becky would never tell a secret, especially if it was meant to be a surprise. "You are gonna die," she said with a laugh. "It just stinks to be you 'cause I am sure as heck not telling," Becky grinned. She was right, I was going to die. Die of curiosity!

"Can you just tell me, please?" I asked with that oh-I-just-gotta-know voice I used so often. "Nope, I am not telling. You have to wait and see," she replied.

This back-and-forth game went on for quite a while as we stood outside the barn washing tack. I was absolutely going mad with curiosity. I had been hoping for the longest time that my parents would get me a horse. I had prayed and wished many times that maybe I would get a horse, any horse, just as long as it had four legs and was at least 10-hands-high. I told myself not to get my hopes up, for the chances of me getting a horse were very, very slim.

I asked my mom that day while driving home if she knew anything about the mysterious secret Becky had stored away in her head. "No, I have no clue what Becky is talking about," my mother replied. My hopes were once again dashed, and I turned to face the window, still hoping just a tiny bit that maybe it was a horse for me.

Days later, I stepped off the bus and was greeted with the welcoming scent of horses, the perfect combination of odors to make me feel at home. I glanced with interest at the smallest paddock containing the new filly, Bailey.

"Hello, Bailey darling," I said with love. My friends, Devon and Mandy, excitedly joined me in petting her. They had come with me to the barn for our riding lesson. My riding instructor's car was there, but there was no sign of Becky. "Hey you guys!" Yelled the barn owner from in the barn. "There's a baby rabbit in the stall hiding on me. Come up here and help me get it out!"

Devon, Mandy and I ran up to the barn, concerned about the rabbit. As we approached, Lu urged us to hurry. She pointed to the first stall and said, "In here. I think he's hiding on us." We all stepped slowly into the stall, keeping our eyes open for any sign of the rabbit. "Aw, shoot! It must have gotten away," stated Lu after several minutes of tedious searching and shushing from Devon, who insisted that the noise would flush the rabbit out.

Mandy, Devon and I all glanced at each other. We knew what came next: work. "Okay, Alissa, you go get Liz. Mandy, you get Sunny and Devon, you can help with the gate." We all hastily grabbed halters and lead ropes, because whatever Lu says, goes.

As we clamored down the hill leading to the paddocks, laughing and wondering about the rabbit, Becky and my mom appeared around the corner of our tack room. They were leading a beautiful black horse with a white "J" on her forehead. Just as I was going to ask who the horse was, Becky said, "Alissa, meet your horse, J.J." My heart seemed to stop as I tried to comprehend what Becky was saying.

"*My* horse?" I asked meekly as Becky handed me the lead rope. Mandy and Devon were screeching to express their excitement.

"She's a purebred six-year-old Arabian mare, and you'll be leasing her for a year," Becky announced. I was barely listening, because I was so happy, but somehow all the information got implanted in my brain. It was sort of like spilling black ink on a brilliant white carpet. It isn't coming out anytime soon.

I felt a lot like a little boy getting his first brand new bike - extremely happy and completely speechless. I knew from then on, J.J. and I could never be separated.

But I just had one question:

What the heck happened to that darn rabbit?

Alissa Ricci

Biography - Alissa Ricci. "I am 13-years-old and I live in Rhode Island. One of my favorite hobbies besides horseback riding and writing is drawing. I draw mostly horses (go figure!) but I also enjoy landscapes. I have a great family: my parents, and my two younger brothers. But I also have another family, my barn family. They consist of all the kids and adults I am associated with at Pondview Stables. They are the greatest people I know and I thank them all for their support. I have one horse, which I am leasing for a year, hopefully more, named J.J. She is a great animal and has given me so much to look forward to for the next year."

Rusty Was My First Horse

During the summer that I was in the fifth grade, my parents signed me up for a horse day camp. I just couldn't get enough. My best friend and I would get up at five thirty in the morning and make my mom, or her mom, take us to the ranch. The first campers to arrive got first pick of the horses they would have for that day. If you were late, you ended up with what was left, and of course we couldn't have that.

I remember the first day of camp. My mom picked us up at the end of the day and we were covered from head to foot with the smell of horse. There was some discussion that night about not allowing us to go back to a camp that would let two little girls get into such a condition in the first place. My dad said, "Don't worry about them; smelling like a horse is an honor. Did you know that the time you spend with a horse will be added on to the end of your life?"

That summer, I discovered my dad had always loved horses. He would be sure to ask about my day and I would tell him what horse I had ridden and where we went and every thing that happened - even the bad stuff. Now that I think about it, I guess that was the summer my dad and I became good friends.

We ended up being able to stay in camp for the rest of the summer. I couldn't believe how much work there was on a horse ranch. There were 30 horses and we had to feed them all and clean their stalls before we could ride each day. Mostly we rode bareback, except for the days when we went off the ranch on long rides and on special days when our parents came to the camp to check on our progress.

By the end of that summer, I could ride all the horses on the ranch, and even saddle my own horse with the help of a stepladder we all used.

By the end of each day, I had a hard time staying awake for dinner; I don't think I watched television at all that summer.

Just before the end of the camp season, I told my dad I didn't think I could make it all the way until next year without horses in my life. He assured me that the world wouldn't end if I didn't go riding for a few months. Little did I know that he had already made arrangements to buy me a horse.

The first Friday after I started back to school, my dad picked me up after classes and told me we were going to take a ride out to the ranch to say hi to my horsey friends. When we got there, I walked around the barn saying hi to all my pals. I noticed there was a new horse in the end stall where the owner used to keep his horse. I walked over and read the plaque on the stall door. It said, "Rusty" and under that was *my name*. My heart got stuck in my throat and I could feel tears coming to my eyes. I was afraid to ask if the name on the plaque meant that this was my horse. I looked up at my dad and he said, "Do you like him?"

Then I knew. This was my horse and he was beautiful, even more beautiful now than he was a few minutes earlier. He was a 14-year-old chestnut with a flaxen mane and tail. He was 14.3-hands and a little on the chunky side. But I knew how to cure that; a little work and he would be back in shape in no time at all.

This is where the story gets very hard to tell. My dad asked me to come and sit down. He wanted to talk to me about Rusty. He told me that when they came to pick Rusty up from the farm he was at before, there was an accident. The trailer they used to move him had a bad floorboard and Rusty's hoof went through the floor and he hurt himself when he tried to pull his foot back out. I asked if he was going to be all right. My dad told me that the vet was coming in the morning and we would know better then. It didn't matter to me - I wouldn't care if he only had three legs, he was my horse and I'd make sure he got better. I asked if I could take him out and look at him and my dad said, "Sure, he could use a good brushing and a carrot or two."

143

I spent the next hour or so using everything I learned all summer long to make him look just right. I found that special spot every horse has and scratched him there for a minute or two and we became fast friends. He put his head down and I looked into those big brown eyes and told him that I loved him and he would be safe from now on. My dad said, "Okay, sweetheart, it's time to go. Let's get Rusty back in his stall for the night."

On the ride home, I made a list of things we were going to need for Rusty. Of course, everything had to be purple and would have to have his name on it. I couldn't wait to get home and call all my friends and tell them about my new horse. When we walked into the house my mom was smiling from ear to ear and gave me a great big hug and told me what a lucky girl I was to have a dad like that.

The next morning, my dad met the vet at the ranch who examined Rusty. He told my dad that it was too early to tell much; in a couple of weeks we'd know better what to expect. He gave us some pain pills and gave Rusty a shot so his shoulder wouldn't get inflamed. The vet told my dad that this was the second horse that was hurt in that trailer and advised him that he should make sure the owner of the ranch paid the vet bill and stopped using the trailer until he fixed it. That was the last day Rusty spent at the ranch. My dad had him moved to a better stable closer to where we lived and made sure the owner paid the vet bill before he left. I never asked him what happened that morning. I was just happy that Rusty was in a beautiful stable now.

A month and two vet visits later, we got the bad news: Rusty had dislocated his shoulder in the accident and would be out of commission for a year or so. The x-rays were conclusive; the vet said Rusty would probably need to take it easy for the rest of his life.

I can't remember much about what happened the next week or so. Dad and I would go out to the stable every other day and I would take Rusty for a walk and brush him and give him carrots and we'd go home. The following Saturday, my best friend's father bought her one of the horses that was for sale at the stable where Rusty was. I tried to be happy for her, but it was very hard.

That same day, I saw my dad talking to a lady who kept her horse in the same barn Rusty was in. They walked over to me and the lady said, "Your dad was telling me the story about Rusty. I think I have some good news for you, young lady." She told us that she was moving that week to a place where she couldn't take her horse. "It would make me very happy if you would consider taking Ivory as your own horse. I watch you walk your horse and have those long talks with him all the time and I know that you'll love Ivory just as much some day."

I was very excited, yet very sad. How would I tell Rusty that I had a new horse already, and what would happen to him? I knew my parents couldn't afford to keep two horses. Later that afternoon, our vet came out to the farm to see another horse. He congratulated me on my new horse. "I was wondering what your plans for Rusty are?" He asked. "I'm interested, because a good friend of mine is looking for a companion horse for his 18-year-old mare. She just retired this year and she needs company. He has a beautiful farm and Rusty would get the best of care. Both he and his wife are vets and love horses." My dad said, "What do you think, sweetheart? It sounds like a wonderful solution, especially for Rusty."

I spent the rest of that day saying good-bye to my first horse. I'm 18 now and when my dad told me he was going to write this story, my heart leapt into my throat and tears welled up in my eyes just as they did the day I got Rusty. You never stop loving your first horse, I guess.

Dale J. Fraza

Biography - Dale J. Fraza. "I am a 55-year-old barn builder. I have been involved with horses for most of my life. I live on an 11-acre horse farm and raise Arabian,/Warmblood crosses. I decided to take up writing this past January and this is my first effort. I'm working on a novella at the present time and I am planning a novel about horses soon."

Misti

When I started riding, Misti was six months old or a little bit more. I was five, soon to turn six in a few days. I started riding at this particular farm because Becca, my riding instructor, placed an ad for a beginners' riding camp. My mother signed me up for it. When I arrived, I was so surprised at what I saw. Horses and kids everywhere. I thought it was the most amazing thing ever.

I met a nice tall girl named Macayla and she took me up to the barn to help get ready. There were a few girls there who were about my age and it looked like we were in the same situation, because all of us looked like we didn't know what in the world was going on. There were some kids that *did* know what was going on and they were running around with tack, trying to saddle up different horses. There wasn't much room in the barn, so I just stepped outside. There I saw a big, fat bay horse in her paddock. I took a second look only to find a little horse alongside her. I had never seen a horse that small before. Since I was too small and unprepared for helping with the horses, I had nothing to do, so I went over to the paddock and attempted to pet the tiny horse. Because she was so young and had not been handled much, she shied away from me. Another thing that kept me from touching that beautiful animal was the mother. She didn't know me, so she wasn't sure if I was going to hurt her baby.

In a few minutes it was time for me to start my lesson. I was so excited. I was so young that I didn't know that there were some horses that you couldn't ride. Not knowing this, I asked Becca if instead of riding the snowy white pony, could I ride the little one in the paddock. She looked at me and laughed. She tried to explain to me why I couldn't ride that horse. "That is Misti, and she is much too young to be ridden yet."

From that day on, whenever I came to the barn to ride, I would always give Misti a carrot. When I came up one day, they were loading Misti into the trailer. But she wasn't that little anymore. I had been riding at the barn for about two years and was older, more mature, and had a lot better grasp on what was going on at the barn. I even owned a little pony named Beau at that time.

As they were loading Misti into the trailer, it was just my natural instinct to ask what was going on. Becca's mother, Lu, said "Misti is going for training." I didn't want her to leave, but what could I do about it?

She was gone for three months. Lu had to go and check on her, and she asked me if I would like to come and ride her. I almost screamed with joy! It was a long drive, but it was well worth it. When we got there, someone was warming her up. She was moving beautifully. It meant a lot to me that I would be allowed to ride her. I couldn't wait; it felt like everything in my body was jumping around.

For the half hour I rode Misti, I felt as if I was in a dream. On the ride home, Lu mentioned that Misti was for sale. I started thinking about what it would be like to own Misti. What about Beau? What was I going to do with him? I asked Lu about this and she told me not to worry about it, and that we could talk to my parents about Misti first, then if they decided to get her, we could find a nice home for Beau. That comforted me for a while.

My parents agreed to let me have Misti. I was *so* excited. The next step was to find a perfect home for Beau. That killed me. After several people looked at him, Lu said, "Why don't I buy Beau? That way, we can use him for lessons and shows!" That was the perfect solution - my two favorite horses at the same barn.

Beau had the best home in the world and best of all, I could see him every time I went to the barn. Misti and I had just started our new partnership. Our first year of showing was the greatest year of my life! We competed in walk-trot and did really well. My little mare loves to jump, so we did some jumping classes. Not too much, though, because she was still very young.

Now it is the winter of 2001. In a few weeks, Misti and I will be getting awards for the success we had in the show season of 2000. We are champion in walk-trot, walk-trot equitation, and placed third in halter. During the show season of 2001, Misti and I are going to be competing in walk-trot-canter. I am really excited about that and I can't wait!

Mandy Soter

Biography - Mandy Soter. Mandy is 12-years-old and now owns a four-year-old Half-Arab, which she hopes to show in Arabian shows. Her favorite classes at school are language and literature. Mandy started riding at the age of six.

April's Easter Dawn

With windchills in the 20-below zero range, and a strong, gusty wind whirling snow crystals around the blackness outside, the barn was an eerie place to spend the night. On that cold March evening, lying beside my husband in the warmth of a bed would have been my preference.

But fate had made a different choice. Our 12-year-old bay Appendix Quarter Horse mare, Nikki, lay dying. There was nothing more the vet could do. He had wanted to give her one more day, as her vital organs hadn't yet started shutting down, and he was still holding on to the hope that she could turn around. Nikki was wrapped in blankets, moaning with every breath. My prayers had changed from, "Dear Lord, please save my Nikki," to "Dear Lord, please end this dear friend's suffering." At 4:15 that March 7th morning, God honored my request. With one last deep sigh, my dear Nikki was gone.

Losing Nikki took more out of me than many of my friends could understand. If you have never lost a horse, or if you have never owned one, it may not be possible to comprehend the emotions that crash inside of you. One moment I would be fine, and the next I would catch a scent or envision a scene that would bring Nikki back to life - only to realize that she was gone forever. No longer would I stroke her mane, kiss her nose, plan her training in the quietness of her stall, laying it all out, so sure she was understanding everything. Nikki was just gone, untouchable, unreachable - gone. There were days when I believed her death really was my fault. I would play out the scene to my husband, and he would gently remind me of all the reasons her death could not possibly have been caused by me.

There were the dreams with Nikki coldly staring at me, accusing me of not trying hard enough, of not fighting enough for her sake. And then there were the times I wept out of pure sadness and loneliness.

The other horses were my comfort. My husband, Dennis, has always teased me about having to have all the stalls filled in our barn. The stalls were all filled now, except Nikki's. Ruby, our Buckskin mare, was due to foal in a month's time, and that would help. Not only would I soon have a little one to fill that stall, but my time would be filled, too, with all the work that goes into raising a foal.

Time passed and Ruby became rounder as the days grew longer. My prayers of frustration and grief turned to prayers of hope and continuing life. "Dear God," I prayed, "Please allow me the opportunity to see this little one into life. Please protect Ruby and her baby from harm, and send me the light needed for this dark heart I am carrying now."

As Ruby approached her due date, she became more restless and obviously uncomfortable. Because Ruby was a maiden mare, I kept a very close eye on her, not knowing her personal signs of impending labor. There continued to be no waxing up, not much bagging, and only a small amount of relaxing around the perineal area. It was going to be a long and frustrating wait.

The evening before Easter, as the horses were being fed, Ruby seemed a little more nervous and a little less comfortable. Nothing else much had changed. I went back to the house to enjoy the evening with my family. We stayed up later than usual, so at 11:30 p.m. I ran back out to the barn for one more check. Ruby wasn't too impressed with this nighttime disturbance and definitely wanted me gone. With a sigh of disappointment, I headed back to the house.

Everyone else was settled in for the night. Climbing into bed, I dozed off. Being a sound sleeper, I usually enjoy a full night's sleep, but not on this particular night. Suddenly I was sitting upright in bed. My heart was pounding and I had lost sense of where I was. I gasped for air as Dennis awoke to comfort me. "You must have been having a bad dream," he assured me. "Lay down and relax. Everything is okay."

I lay back down, but everything did not seem okay. My heart continued to race. Suddenly, it came to me . . . I shouted, "It's Ruby! She is in labor! Come to the barn." I didn't look back as I threw on clothes and ran. I knew Dennis would follow, and he did.

We stepped out into a cool, windless night. The stars were bright and the air was still. Reaching the barn door, my pace slowed. Taking a deep breath to settle my nerves, I quietly slid open the barn door. From the doorway, all I could see was Ruby standing, her head lowered slightly, perhaps in sleep? Was I wrong? As my husband joined me and we walked to the stall, joy filled my soul. Ruby was in the late stages of labor! We quietly found a dark corner and waited as Ruby gave birth to a beautiful tri-colored filly.

I looked at my watch to see the face of time staring back at me, reading just what it had on that bitterly cold night Nikki had breathed her last. I looked at my husband with tears in my eyes and said, "Today is the seventh, and it is 4:15." It was exactly one month from the moment Nikki had left me. The significance of the moment struck us both. This April day, as the dawning of the sun brought in Easter morning, life was renewed. "April's Easter Dawn" struggled to her feet, and after a few wobbly falls, she made her way to mamma. The barn was filled with the sounds of a suckling foal. I bowed my head and uttered a prayer of thanks.

Melinda Strimback-Pepper

Biography - Melinda Strimback-Pepper. "I grew up in the country and inherited my love for horses from my Dad. My best and earliest memories are of the horses I loved and the man I learned that love from. From Dad I learned my love of barrel racing and training young horses. When I found the man I wanted to marry, my only demand was that he share my love of horses, and he has. We have two children, and the four of us enjoy running at barrel shows. We also camp with my parents and our horses and we spend many enjoyable hours trail riding together. We live in the country outside a very small town and share our home with five horses, two dogs, and a barn cat."

One Or The Other

Clint has been on horses since before he could hold his head up, so naturally his father and I felt as if he would always be a rider, because he loved it so much. When Clint's pony, Dixie, suffered a massive stroke a couple of years ago, we thought Clint was slowly weaning himself from riding after the pain of losing his "girl", as he called her.

Christmas arrived and both his father, Kim, and I believed Clint would like a horse of his own. He had been riding Baldy, one of the ranch horses, and wanted to go to some shows. Before Dixie died, Clint and the old pony ran barrels at the Odessa Ranch Rodeo for kids, and he would help us gather cows with her.

Sometimes, one of the ranch hands would have to ride Baldy and Clint had to stay home, so he was getting to the point where he was losing interest. We surprised him with a nice bay Quarter Horse gelding and although Clint liked him, I could tell right away that he did not click with him as he had with Dixie.

As the months went by, it was soon time to work the cows and calves, but Clint did not want to help. Some of the happiest times I have had are watching Clint riding beside his dad and the guys, hunting down cows and checking the rest of the pasture while I rode drag, or whatever they asked me to do.

When April arrives and it is Odessa Rodeo time, everyone around here is happy to see it. The rodeo is just about the biggest thing that happens in Odessa. Clint always loved to ride in the Grand Entry.

Since I ride for the Drill Team and we open each of the rodeo performances, he could ride every night if he wanted to, but sadly, he was not interested. Clint came along to practice with me, but just sat around. He did not want to take his new horse and I could tell how badly he missed the pony.

My friend, Cheryl, brought a pony to practice one afternoon for her daughter's friend to ride around. Clint was watching the pony like a hawk. I later remarked to Cheryl that it was too bad the pony, whose name was Tina, was not for sale. It turned out that the boarder who owned the pony *did* want to sell her, because their son had lost interest. I told Kim over supper that night and the natural answer was that we did not need another horse until the current one left. I could agree with that, but Clint was disappointed. "Let's go see her," Kim suggested.

Clint was already headed to the barn to get his saddle. Clint rode the pony all around Cheryl's barn, yard and house. I saw that same magical combination that had existed with Dixie, so we bought Tina.

One day at a schooling show, Clint saw some kids jumping in another field and really liked the idea. Clint and I would build small jumps out on the trails made of fallen trees and brush and pretend we were cross-country jumping. We also made some low jumps out of PVC pipe and he would jump in my little close-contact saddle all around the yard. Clint has a natural ability as a rider and Tina also showed some talent.

I thought Kim would "wig" when Clint received breeches as a birthday gift. We have a wonderful friend who trains jumpers and she worked with Tina and Clint for three months. Kim even thought they were pretty good, "but can't he wear *jeans*?" It was about this time that Clint started to express an interest in computers, and because of the expense was told it was "one or the other" - his pony or the land of high technology.

Cheryl told us about a Western speed circuit in San Antonio, Florida, in which her daughter was running, and thought that Clint might be interested. Not only did we all have a super fun night, but Clint and Tina ended up winning the High Point award for his age division. He ran barrels, poles, Texas barrels, the hair pin and arena race. I know in my heart that Tina, who had no experience with any of this that I know of prior to this show, ran for Clint because of his talent and the confidence that he conveys to a pony that loves him dearly. Clint finished the five-month circuit by winning the Reserve Champion belt buckle for his age division.

Clint's dad and I are so proud of him for his accomplishments, and all the hard work he does taking care of his pony, even when he did not care much about riding, and for being a good sport.

He did tell me he was glad he did not trade Tina for a computer!

Mona L. Malone

Biography - Mona L. Malone. "I am married and have two boys: Justin. 18, and Clint, 13. We have four horses, three dogs and three cats. We live on the Anclote River Ranch (3400 acres) located in Odessa, Florida, where my husband Kim is the ranch foreman. The ranch was mainly a commercial cow/calf operation and has now branched out to the eco-tourism industry, where we give guided tours. We are involved in barrel racing, reining, working cow horses, and starting and training our own colts. I thank God for the beauty around me and the gift of writing."

Dreams Can Come True

I have always wanted my own horse and thanks to the Make-A-Wish Foundation, I now have one. Here is how it happened.

On June 16th, 2000, my last day of fourth grade, I went for my yearly physical. When the doctors were checking my stomach area, they found something that wasn't supposed to be there, so they said I would have to have a CATscan to see what it was. Later that day, the CATscan was performed. My family and I were called into my pediatrician's office that night and told that there was a mass on my kidney. I would need surgery right away. My doctor had arranged for us to meet with the surgeon on Monday the 19th at Children's Hospital in Boston.

We didn't sleep much that weekend. Finally, Monday arrived and it was time to meet Dr. Shamberger, the surgeon. He told us that I would need surgery to remove the tumor and my kidney. He explained to us what was going to happen during the surgery on Wednesday. I was admitted to Children's Hospital on Tuesday morning, and had more x-rays and CATscans. That night I had to drink a gallon of Go-Litely, which is a drink that cleans out your intestines. I tried to drink it, but it didn't taste very good. I tried twice but couldn't keep it down, so they had to stick a tube down my nose to get the liquid in my stomach. It wasn't a very fun night. I was very nervous and very worried. My Mom stayed with me at the hospital and she tried to keep my mind off of the surgery.

On Wednesday, I had the surgery. It took almost seven hours to remove my kidney, because the tumor was the size of a large cantaloupe, and to implant a port-a-cath into my chest (which is where they administered the chemo into my body). While I was in recovery, the surgeon told my parents that he believed that I had Wilms' Tumor, which is a childhood cancer of the kidney.

I wasn't able to walk for four days after the surgery. My left leg was numb from the painkillers. The nurses (my favorite one was Jennifer) made me move into a chair every day to get the blood circulating in my legs. The day following the surgery, it took my parents and two nurses nearly an hour to move me into a chair because of the pain and all of the tubes I had attached to me for pain medicine, fluids, etc. Finally after a few days, I was able to walk, so they let me go home. Before I left the hospital the tumor was officially diagnosed as Wilms' Tumor. Everyone kept saying how lucky I was to only have Wilms' Tumor, because it is a very treatable kind of cancer . . . but I didn't feel very lucky!

After being home for a few days, my chemo started at the Dana Farber Cancer Institute/Jimmy Fund Clinic in Boston. Everyone was really nice at the Jimmy Fund. I had to go for a chemotherapy treatment once a week for ten weeks, and then once every three weeks until November. Once I started the chemo, I asked my doctor when I could ride horses again, and he said I would have to wait a few months. This made me so mad, because I felt well enough to ride and because I love to ride horses. So I kept getting my chemo, resting, and thinking about the day when I could ride again.

The chemo made me very sick and tired, made food taste funny, and I started to lose my hair. Every few weeks I had to have chest x-rays and an ultrasound to make sure that the cancer wasn't coming back. It wasn't a very fun summer for me. There weren't many days that I felt well enough to run around and play with my friends.

Finally, in the middle of August, my doctor said I could ride again. A few days later I had a riding lesson. I rode the smallest pony there, and had to wear a vest for protection and take it a lot easier than usual. It was really boring. I was used to cantering and going over little jumps, but now all I could do was walk. Despite such a slow pace, I loved being back on a horse again! I continued to ride weekly after that.

In October, my parents got a call from the Make-A-Wish Foundation (which grants wishes to children with life-threatening illnesses) and they said that they would like to visit and find out what my wish was. I knew right away what would make me the happiest little girl in the world - a horse! Diane and Mike, my wish granters, came over and I told them that my wish was to own a horse. I had to have a backup wish in case they couldn't get me a horse, so I told them that my second choice was a trip to Ridin'-Hy Ranch in Warrensburg, New York. My family goes there every year during winter vacation and I love it there.

It took Diane, Mike and Barbara (the executive director of the New Hampshire Make-A-Wish Foundation) two long weeks to get back to us. They came over one night with some gifts and told me that they were searching for the perfect horse for me. I couldn't believe it - I was going to get a horse! I could barely sleep that night, because I was dreaming of my horse! What would it look like? I couldn't wait to tell my teacher and my friends.

I had my last chemo treatment on November 2nd. I always felt nervous and sick to my stomach when I had to go for my treatments, but not this time, because I was thinking about my horse. I managed to go to school part-time while I was having my treatments, and I drove my teacher crazy because everything I wrote was about horses!

On November 20, my parents said that they had arranged for me to take a riding lesson after lunch. My 13-year-old sister, Jennica, and my Grandma Bradley came along, too. When we got to the barn, the people from Make-A-Wish were there along with Kathy and Dawn (my riding instructors). First, they had me open presents. I got a saddle, a bridle, and all of the stuff I would need to own a horse. I wasn't sure what was going to happen next. I didn't think they were going to give me the horse then, but I was happy that they got me all the equipment so when I did get a horse, I would have everything I needed.

After I finished opening all the presents, Kathy and my Dad opened the barn doors. Standing there in a stall, looking at me, was the most beautiful horse in the world, a leopard Appaloosa mare named Charlie's Redford (a.k.a. Cher), and a sign saying, "Cher - I'm Cecily's Horse." I was so shocked! I wasn't quite sure what to say. I went into her stall and started patting her. Cher seemed very calm and she let everybody touch her. I took her out, because everyone wanted to take pictures.

Soon after, everyone left except my Mom, Dad, sister, my friend Kristi, and my Grandma. My teacher, Miss Adams, and my gym teacher, Miss Long, also came to see Cher. I walked her around and my Mom helped me brush her. We finally put her in her stall and one of the barn workers brought her dinner to her. After she ate, we left. On our way home, we were all talking about how great it was that I had a horse and everything I would need to take care of her.

Later that night, I called my family and friends to tell them the news of my horse. Everyone I called was very excited that my wish had come true. I told my Mom that I would go through the surgery and chemo all over again just for a horse.

On November 24th, I had another ultrasound and the doctor declared me "essentially disease free." My Mom, dad, Jennica and I celebrated by going to Bertucci's for pizza. I had surgery to remove the port-a-cath in December. I had to wait a week - which seemed like forever - after that surgery before I could ride again.

I ride Cher almost every day. I either ride in the ring, on the trails, or in the field. Some days I just walk Cher around and talk to her. She is my best friend and I love her as much as I love my family. I also compete in local competitions. In my first competition, I won two blue ribbons for equitation and going over trotting poles. I'm not allowed to jump yet. I can't wait for the doctor to give me his okay to jump. In June, on my 11th birthday, I am going on a trail ride to raise money for the New Hampshire Make-A-Wish Foundation. I want to make sure that another girl or boy can have their wish come true, just like I did.

Cecily Bradley

Biography - Cecily Bradley is 11-years-old and a fifth grader at Broad Street Elementary School in Nashua, New Hampshire. She loves to ride horses and hopes to be a trainer someday. Cecily takes riding lessons at Kilkenny Horse Center in Hollis, NH. Riding is her favorite thing to do, and she is always telling her sister "Who needs friends when you have a horse!"

"Most of the important things in the world have been accomplished by people who have kept on trying when there seemed to be no hope at all."

Dale Carnegie

Horse Tales for the Soul
Volumes One and Two

Cover designed by
Kromatiks Graphic Design

Specializing in Graphics for the Equine Industry

Advertising

Stallion Promotion

Book, Video & Magazine Cover Art

Photo Composite Portraits & Photo Retouching

Web Site Design

for information Contact:
Kristen Spinning
(520) 760-0388
krisspin@aol.com

Thank you to all the writers who contributed photos for this cover.
It was hard to choose just a few. - Kris